VOICE IN THE MIRROR

WILL THE FINAL APOCALYPSE BE AVERTED?

BY

LEE SHARGEL, PH.D.

THE FIRST BOOK OF THE CHULOSIAN CHRONICLES

Inner Eye Books

An Imprint of
OUGHTEN HOUSE PUBLICATIONS
LIVERMORE, CALIFORNIA, USA

Voice in the Mirror: Will The Final Apocalypse Be Averted?
by
Lee Shargel, Ph.D.
Published 1997

01 00 99 98 97   0 9 8 7 6 5 4 3 2

PUBLISHED BY:
INNER EYE BOOKS
an imprint of
OUGHTEN HOUSE PUBLICATIONS
P.O. BOX 2008
LIVERMORE, CALIFORNIA, 94551-2008 USA
PHONE: (510) 447-2332
FAX: (510) 447-2376
E-MAIL: Oughtenhouse@rest.com

Library of Congress Cataloging-in-Publication Data

Shargel, Lee, 1950–
        Voice in the mirror: will the final apocalypse be averted? / by Lee Shargel.
                p.   cm.   -- (The Chulosian chronicles ; 1st)
        ISBN 1-880666-54-5 (hardcover)
        I. Title. II Series: Shargel, Lee 1950–   Chulosian chronicles ;   1st
        PS3569.H3426V65   1996
        813' .54--dc21
                                                                        96–49398
                                                                        CIP

ISBN 1-880666-54-5, Hardcover Cloth Edition
Printed in United States of America

DEDICATION

For my wife Deborah, who never stops believing, and my son Jason-Lee. I would also like to thank the internationally acclaimed author with an "Instinct," Robert W. Walker, a good friend and teacher whose valued instruction helped me make this book possible.

And to the memory of Dr. Helene Walczak, who first taught me how to put it down on paper.

To Robert Gerard at Oughten House for taking a chance at the beginning and helping with the ending.

And a good "*new*" friend, Tony Stubbs, for the inspiring editing and advice well taken.

Can't forget my old friends at Hudson Tool & Die Company. Rick Pfluger, Ray Michaels, Paul Clare (with whom the story was born on the way to Tampa—Testeverdeeeee!) and Ed Moniot, Tom Coles and Joe Hynes.

To all of my pals at Telectronics—*Caramba!*

And to my friends at NASA for their help in bringing the truth to fiction—Science Fiction!

FOREWORD

Kennedy Space Center, Florida.

The events that have taken place since the launch of the Hubble Space Telescope, its subsequent failure due to a manufacturing flaw in its mirrors, and the COSTAR mission that followed have given rise to many questions.

Does the telescope really have the ability to look into mankind's past? Can scientists peer into the vastness of outer space and view the birth and death of stars? What do we hope to learn from this celestial experiment that has cost taxpayers billions of dollars? And let's not forget the questions that have plagued mankind for over a generation. Does life exist on other planets? And if so, will we ever discover them? Have they already discovered us? Could the Hubble Telescope be the link in a cosmic telecommunications superhighway? Are we on-line right now?

The United States Government has a policy dating back to the incident at Roswell that states that if and when contact is made with an alien civilization, it shall, for reasons of national security, social and religious ethics, and most importantly, the concerns of the medical community, remain Top Secret, indefinitely. This policy has kept the real truth from the American people. It is classified at a level even higher than the Manhattan Project during World War II, and it is presently the most closely guarded secret in our nation. Are they correct, though, in their assumption that the human race is still not prepared for interaction with benign alien beings? Are we still so violently prehistoric in our prejudiced view of others that face to face contact with them would result in conflict?

In the ancient book of Genesis it is written that after man was created he was placed in the Garden. Who created man in the first place? Are we on Earth some alien civilization's experiment in genetic engineering? Could our development as a race of beings be a living testament to some other more ancient culture? Are they studying us in the hope of learning of their own origin? Is planet Earth just a large Jurassic Park?

Maybe they are scientists too, celestial paleontologists in search of their own roots. Have they already been here searching for answers to questions we have yet to ask? Perhaps they may be like our own historical explorers who, in the late nineteenth century, ventured into the unexplored jungles of Africa, captured primitive tribes-people, brought them back to civilization for study, and then returned them to the wild. What would these primitive people have thought of our modern civilization and how could their primitive beliefs explain it? How would contact with a more technologically advanced civilization change them? And what would we do if our science knew of an impending threat to their survival and could prevent their destruction but only by overturning those same primitive beliefs? What are the obligations of an advanced culture towards a more primitive one? Save them at any cost but destroy their culture, or stand by and let their destiny unfold without our interference?

Voice in the Mirror explores these timely questions. You, the reader, must find meaning for yourself within the answers. Our planet is not alone in the vast cosmic ocean of space. Nor can we be so presumptuous as to believe that we are the only race of intelligent beings adrift in that great cosmic sea. There is proof that we have been in contact with an alien culture, and are in contact with them now. The Hubble Telescope, powerful now that its vision has been corrected, enables us to look far into the distant past and also into the future. We have witnessed the birth and death of stars, and cosmic collisions with celestial bodies. As we send out greetings from Earth, is it so implausible that some other civilization may be doing the same thing?

With UFO sightings becoming commonplace, and tales of alien abduction becoming more plausible, are we at last on the threshold of a new awakening? Could the Hubble Telescope be the conduit that enables us to make that first real contact? Could it be the cellular picture-phone in orbit above our planet that takes the first call? If so, then perhaps one of our distant neighbors has already dialed the number.

The galactic phone is ringing. Are we ready to answer?

— Lee Shargel

PROLOGUE

April 25, 1990, 3:38 p.m.

The space shuttle *Discovery* successfully launches the Hubble Space Telescope (HST). Scientists and engineers at NASA cheer the sight of the huge cylinder gliding into orbit 380 miles above the Earth. The future of astronomy and a new era in the study of Earth's origin has begun.

***

The executive conference room at the Parkin-Eldred Corporation was filled to standing room only. Men and women, some of the company's top executives, were seated around the big oval table. At the head of the table was Michael Cason, Vice-President of Operations. He stood amidst the clamor and jubilation and cleared his throat. As he rose to address his audience, two men standing at the back of the room exchanged a nervous glance. A look of deep concern flowed between them, even though they did their best to conceal their emotions. But with all of the clamor and excitement of the moment, no one noticed their worrisome exchange.

The telescope had been deployed and was about to make astronomical history. The Parkin-Eldred Corporation had constructed the mirrors used on the scope and it was time to celebrate their achievement. For Mike Wooten and Phil Lombardo, the two engineers trying desperately to conceal a look of guilt and shame, this was no time for rejoicing. They knew something was seriously wrong with the primary mirror and that it was only a matter of time before the rest of the world knew about it, too.

December 12, 1993

There is an overwhelming fear of being suspended in the weight-lessness of space. Every veteran astronaut knows this. The thought of losing your grip. Of slipping away where they can't reach you. Floating off into the endless darkness that is space. That was the feeling Hank Stanton had as he left the relative safety of the shuttle's cargo bay. The fear of not having anything under your feet was indescribable.

He peered through the visor of his helmet. Slowly he looked down at his feet. Below him, the blackness of space stretched out to infinity. He shook inside his space suit, but he wasn't cold.

The mission, Hank thought, as he touched the keypad on his Manned Maneuvering Unit (MMU), was all that mattered now. He had to overcome this fear or he would 'lose it' completely and fail. The nitrogen thruster on the port side of the MMU fired a short burst of gas. Hank began a slow drift towards the large black tube that was the telescope. The shutter plate that covered the entrance to the telescope was extended upwards. Hank saw a glint of the primary mirror at the center of the cylinder. His companions, Bill Heller and Mark Ramius, both veteran astronauts, were suspended in space at the opening of the telescope. Hank pressed another set of buttons on the MMU keypad and a small braking jet fired and slowed his forward movement. In his left hand he held the Focal Generator.

Hank's grip on the instrument tightened as his right hand con-trolled the keypad on his MMU. He positioned himself over the center of the cylinder and tapped the buttons that activated the port and starboard nitrogen jets on his MMU backpack. The simultaneous fir-ing of the tiny gas rockets propelled him as if in slow motion. He descended into the darkness of the long black tube.

Even with all of his training, Hank felt the walls of the cylinder closing in on him. He immediately switched on the additional fiber-optic lights attached to his MMU. The small beams on the MMU, along with his helmet light, illuminated the interior of the telescope as he descended further. He could hear himself breathing as the exhaust made a hissing sound inside his helmet.

At the rim of the Hubble cylinder, the other two astronauts both gave the thumbs-up signal to Hank as they watched him glide down along the edge inside the telescope.

"How's it look, Hank?" Mark Ramius' voice crackled through the ear phones in Hank's helmet.

"I can see the Low Light Spectrographic Gyro. I just have to move the High Speed Photometer and the generator should fit nicely between them."

"Textbook, Hank. Just like we rehearsed at the Cape," Bill Heller replied.

The sound of breathing reverberated through their headphones and sounded like the sucking sound of a filling popping out of a tooth, Hank thought as he continued his descent past the support structure of the secondary mirror. He again tapped at the center button on the MMU keypad and his momentum was stopped by the small braking jet. He remained suspended in the center of the space telescope, just above the primary mirror.

Hank was on his own now. The TV and voice link to the ground was turned off for this part of the mission. Only a handful of people were aware of the additional unit being fitted into the equipment bay of the HST.

"Looks like a perfect fit," Hank said, snapping the instrument in place and pressing the power-on button.

A series of green lights illuminated the small panel indicating that the unit was functioning normally. Hank looked down at the large primary mirror, the glint of a million stars reflecting off its polished surface. Like diamonds on a felt cloth in a jewelry store, he thought.

A blinking light on the keypad turned his attention away from the mirror. He glanced at the digital readout panel attached to his wrist. The time elapsed indicator told him that this mission was taking longer than anticipated. Hank tilted his body ever so slightly in his space suit. The motion was just enough to cause him to rotate backwards, almost as if he were going to do a back flip. Ramius and Heller came into view at the opening above. Hank saw them both give the thumbs-up sign again. He returned the gesture.

Suddenly a pin point of bright light appeared in the center of the primary mirror.

"Hey! Wait a minute. What the hell's going on here?" Hank exclaimed.

"Hank, you okay?" Mark Ramius asked.

Bill Heller jumped in. "Hank? What's wrong? Mark, stay here I'm going in after—"

"It's not me," Hank interrupted. "It's the damn scope. It's ... the mirror is...well, something's happening to the mirror."

"Hank, what's wrong? I can't see you," Mark Ramius said. He was leaning over further into the cylinder trying to see what was going on below. He noticed the glow as it began to illuminate the inside of the scope. Bill Heller noticed it too as he pulled himself slowly over the edge of the scope. "Hank, where are you? What the hell's going on down there? Bill, come on, we're going in to get Hank," Mark Ramius said with an urgency in his voice.

"Wait!" Hank yelled back. "It's on fire! The primary mirror is on fire! It must be the sun."

The bright light began as a small spot in the center of the mirror and grew by the second in its intensity. Hank was trapped between the superstructure of the primary and secondary mirrors and had no place to go.

The same thought flashed through the minds of all three astronauts simultaneously. "Hank! Hank! We're not in the plane of the sun! The mirror can't be reflecting sunlight!" Ramius yelled to his partner.

"It's on fire!" Hank screamed almost incoherently.

"That's impossible, Hank! Get out of there!" Ramius yelled.

"Use the Safer, Hank! Use the Safer!" Bill Heller called out.

The Safer jetpack was a new device and required on all MMUs. Activated by a thumb switch on the keypad it would instantly propel the astronaut in whatever direction he turned. It was designed to get an astronaut safely back to the shuttle in the event of an emergency if his MMU jets failed.

"Ahhhhhh!"

"Hank! Hank! Are you okay?" Ramius called out.

A blinding light exploded from the center of the scope like a ball of lightning propelling Ramius and Heller away from the cylinder. As suddenly as the light had appeared, it was gone.

"What the hell was that?" Bill Heller asked his partner.

"I don't know. Come on. Let's get Hank."

"What the hell is going on out there? Bill? Mark? Is Hank okay? Should I signal Houston?" reverberated through both astronauts' helmets. It was Colonel Rick Fuller, the shuttle commander. In the confusion, the two astronauts had failed to report in.

"Something's wrong out here, Colonel. Hank is in trouble. Bill and I are descending into the HST," Ramius said.

"Turn on your shoulder cameras. I want to see what's happening out there," Colonel Fuller demanded. The shuttle cockpit was turned away from the telescope. The only way he could monitor the astronauts now was by a closed circuit camera mounted on the shoulder support section of their backpacks.

Ramius and Heller both activated their MMUs and were back at the edge of the telescope in seconds. "Hank! Hank!" they called in unison. No reply.

"I don't see his lights," Ramius replied.

"We're coming in to get you," Heller said, signaling to Ramius to follow him down into the scope. They descended into the Hubble telescope together.

The beams from their helmet lights played over every surface as they slowly moved into the scope.

"Hank?" Bill Heller called.

He reached the primary mirror first and looked over at Ramius, now across the telescope's body from him. They both looked at the reflection of their own disbelief on the glass window of each other's helmet.

"He's gone, Mark. Hank is gone."

September 18, 1992, Goddard Space Flight Center, 2:00 a.m.

The picture of the distant solar system was brilliant in its com-puter-enhanced colors. The new Itech SVGA monitors receiving the signals from the Hubble Space Telescope assembled the bits of data by pixelating them into an 8,000 by 8,000 bisected resolution format. Even Hank, as familiar as he was with this equipment, was still mes-merized at the beauty of the digitized image.

Suddenly, Hank was so startled he nearly choked on the carrot stick dangling from his mouth. He chomped down on it and raced for the keyboard. With a few keystrokes, he set the system to copy mode as a battery of processors and micro-chips began storing the math-ematical symbols and, to his surprise, an unscheduled group of coded images being sent from the HST.

The Vega System: 27 Light Years from Earth

Kamal Tarn stood on the platform, looking down into the Corbal Ring of Infinity. He needed to maintain this thought link as long as possible. The gravity wave through which the signal was traveling might be discovered at any moment. The message he was now sending must be received or the planet would be doomed. He only hoped they would be able to decipher the images before it was too late.

He continued projecting the symbols as he held onto the mental image. The focal generator that powered the Corbal Ring suspended the holographic image of the planet in its center. The thought of step-ping into the ring himself was a tempting idea. Kamal reflected that it had been 12 relons since he was last on the planet. Travel there was now forbidden. One of the planet's species had evolved into a violent race and was to be observed only through the Ring.

As he increased the intensity of his thoughts, the gravity wave in-creased its speed.

Goddard Space Flight Center

"These can't be real," Hank muttered. After being alone in the lab for hours, he talked to the computers as though they were his companions. "Something's got to be wrong here."

Hank pushed the side of the desk with his foot and sent himself and his chair rolling across the lab. He flipped several switches on the Cray 3000, watching the digital readouts. The result of this action was the same. The transmissions being received and analyzed by the computer only confirmed the mystery. Hank pulled away a section of perforated computer paper from the basket at the rear of the line printer and began separating them. With the agility of a Las Vegas blackjack dealer, he spun the bundle over and began scanning each one.

Doctor Henry (Hank) Stanton, described as 'a brilliant and energetic astro-physicist' in *Newsweek* when the Hubble Space Telescope was first deployed, was now busting his hump, working late hours at the Goddard Space Flight Center. He was the leader of a small group of scientists and engineers assigned the command and control functions of the HST, or 'Hub' as it was called by the members of the team.

The 1.5 billion dollar eyepiece in space had proven to be the bane of NASA. The system suffered from technical near-sightedness caused by a flaw in its primary focusing mirror. Although the telescope had its problems, (and a congressional investigation couldn't seem to pinpoint the manufacturer responsible), powerful computer enhancement gave the system about 70% of focal capacity. Still, the scientists were gathering fantastic data from the Milky Way Galaxy and other more remote areas of space despite the technical flaws.

Alone in the lab at 2:00 a.m., Hank was astounded as the computerized system for tracking and analysis electrified the room with a display of digitized pictures from what appeared to be another solar system. Hank did not yet realize that the images coming through the telescope were being sent and received in real time—from a distance of 27 light years.

Cartagay Island Receiving Station in the Pacific Ocean

"Edward, come have a look at this," Doctor Brian McDaniels called to his associate. "What do you suppose is causing this to happen?" he asked, pointing to a screen full of digitized images being received from one of the large antenna dishes positioned around the island.

Professor Edward Devane, recognized around the world as a genius in astronomical science and on loan to NASA from MIT, stepped in from the platform that surrounded the radome. The telemetry equipment for tracking and analysis was housed in the large Geodesic structure.

Doctor McDaniels, a noted astronomer in his own right and on loan to NASA from CALTECH, was glued to a monitor screen in the crowded electronics room. "What have we here now?" asked the professor, standing behind his associate and peering over his shoulder at the monitor.

"You tell me, Edward. I haven't the faintest idea."

The Cartagay Island Receiving Station remained the westernmost listening post for all NASA launches and satellite reception. It was also the secondary orbital telemetry tracking and command transmission point for the Hubble Space Telescope. The military was apt to use the station from time to time to augment the TDRS Terminal at White Sands, New Mexico. Most of the work conducted at Cartagay was classified Top Secret. The public, and most of Congress, were unaware that it even existed. Doctor Brian McDaniels and Professor Edward Devane were engaged in a joint research project studying the blue/white star Vega.

The Hubble had picked up what appeared to be shadows on the surface of the star. These faint images could signify the existence of orbiting planets. McDaniels and Devane, like Stanton and his group, were plagued by the same problem—the flawed mirror distorted images. The COSTAR fix which was being designed and headed up by Doctor Stanton was not slated to be completed for over a year. The scientists' only recourse was computer image enhancement and a good educated guess. Although they were exactly twelve hours apart, both

Cartagay and Goddard were receiving the message from the Hubble at the same time.

"Brian, what's the Wide Field/Planetary Camera's focusing position right now?" Professor Devane asked.

"We should be directly in the plane of Sarius at azimuth 383. The Hubble is looking directly at Vega."

"These symbols can't be coming from the Vega system. That's impossible," Devane replied.

They were both feverishly pushing buttons and throwing switches. Professor Devane never took his eyes off of the computer screen, now scrolling line after line of colorful hieroglyphic-like images. They looked like pictures of Earth, our solar system, a planetary group they had never seen before, and some pictographic images neither of the learned men could immediately decipher.

"What do you make of this?" Brian asked, pointing to a symbol that kept repeating on every other line of data. It was a pictograph of an alien being neither man had ever seen before.

"Brian, if I didn't think I'd be branded a lunatic, I'd say we were receiving a long distance phone call from a star twenty-seven light years from Earth."

Brian McDaniels stared at Professor Devane and then back at the computer monitor. His face suddenly beamed with a wide smile. He turned his attention back to his colleague and with a chuckle said, "By God, Edward. Carl Sagan was right."

Devane looked at McDaniels, perplexed.

"Don't you see, Edward?" Brian exclaimed. "This is the proof! Life! Intelligent life on another planet!"

The Goddard Space Flight Center sits on a sprawling acreage in Greenbelt, Maryland. Its fourteen modern buildings nestled in rolling hills and pine forests and looked like a university campus. Building Four housed the Hubble Telescope Space Science Lab and was at the far end of the neatly manicured grounds. It was surrounded on three sides by trees and six huge satellite dishes that looked like inverted mushrooms in an alien field.

Building Four was Hank Stanton's second home since being assigned to the Hubble research team. Actually, he spent more time there than anyplace else. Today would be no different. At 8:05 a.m., Hank was already in the parking lot getting in his car and preparing for the twenty-minute ride home. Beside him on the passenger seat lay 23 sheets of computer printout from the telescope transmission.

"Good morning, Hank."

Hank was momentarily startled. Instead of placing the key in the car's ignition, he dropped it on the floor under the seat. He turned toward the driver's side window to see Libby Morales, Craig William's secretary.

"Oh...ah...good morning, Libby. You're here early today." He smiled at the young woman while nervously poking around with his right hand under the driver's seat.

"I have some reports for Mister Williams that need to be ready for his nine o'clock meeting," she said, pulling a stack of manila folders from an open shoulder bag.

Hank glanced only briefly at the folders, but long enough to notice that one of them had a red band around it marked TOP SECRET. He glanced up at Libby and forced a smile while still groping for his key ring.

Elizabeth (Libby) Morales was a voluptuous woman of twenty-eight. She had been employed at the lab for only eleven months, but rumor had it that she was hip deep in a torrid love affair with her boss, Craig Williams, Hubble Telescope Project Director. Nothing could have been further from the truth. But Libby was quite pleased with the way things were going, including her clandestine method of planting the hot romance story.

Born in Puerto Rico, she had been raised in the slums of Washington, DC. She received her preliminary education on the streets of the nation's capital. Through hard work and perseverance she had won a scholarship to the prestigious Stapleton Business School for Women. This had more than prepared her for the executive secretary job at the Goddard Flight Center.

"Well…ah…it's nice to see you this morning, Libby, but I really should be getting home. It's been another long night."

Hank found the keys under the seat, picked them up, and inserted the key in the ignition.

Libby gave him a wink and said, "Have a good one, Hank." She turned and began walking towards Building Four and her office.

Hank watched her buttocks rolling gently under her tight red dress. "Hmmm," it's been a long time, he reflected.

As Hank was backing out, he wondered for a moment about the folder in Libby's bag. Since the discovery of the flawed mirror and the congressional investigation that followed, Hank had a suspicion that there was more to the problems with the telescope orbiting Earth. He felt that any proof of wrongdoing was probably beyond his realm of influence.

He turned and looked at the sheets of paper on the passenger seat. He had spent half the night trying to decipher their meaning, but so far he had come up with only more questions. At the moment he was too tired to think of anything but rest. He would get back to the Center later today and pick up where he left off. For the moment, he had better keep this whole incident under wraps until he had some answers. He had scheduled routine maintenance checks to be done on the system for the rest of the day and felt at ease that no one on the team would be checking transmissions today.

"Beep! Beeeeeeeep!"

Hank nearly jumped out of his seat at the sound of the car horn behind him. He hadn't been paying attention and almost backed into Craig Williams' Porsche. Instinctively, he brushed the stack of computer papers onto the passenger floor.

"Doctor Stanton, I wish you would pay more attention to where you're going!" Craig Williams yelled, as he slid his shiny red Porsche into his reserved space.

"Sorry, Craig, long night," Hank replied, and with a wave goodbye, put the car in drive and drove slowly to the guard gate at the entrance to the lab.

Craig Williams retrieved his aluminum Haliburton briefcase from the front seat, closed the car door, and started toward Building Four. Two beeps indicated that the automatic alarm in the Porsche was activated. He turned, looked at the automobile, and smiled. Craig liked the status that the Porsche projected. It demanded respect, he thought to himself as he walked into the building.

"Good morning, Mister Williams," his secretary said with a smile as he entered the office.

"Good morning, Libby." He stopped at the edge of her desk and paused to eye his secretary. He undressed her in his mind for the hundredth time and the lecherous look on his face concealed little of his thoughts.

Libby wore a tight red Spandex dress with a very low neckline that did nothing to hide the cleavage of her ample breasts. The hemline was at least five inches above her knees and the way she sat made it ride up even further.

Craig leaned over the desk and asked if she had completed the reports he needed for his nine o'clock meeting.

"Yes, sir, I made the changes as you requested. They're all right here," she said, handing him the stack of folders on her desk.

He placed his briefcase on the floor and picked up the folders. He casually glanced at the first one and then returned his stare to Libby. "As usual, Libby, you've done an excellent job. I wonder sometimes how I ever got along without you. You know, there's this rumor going around about—"

She interrupted with, "I never pay attention to rumors, Mister Williams."

He looked a little surprised at her remark. He had hoped for a different response. He picked up his briefcase, gave Libby a lascivious smile, and walked around the corner to his office. Libby smiled back and muttered *"bendayho."* Ordinarily, no executive secretary would dress so blatantly, but Libby thought this would be an excellent way to manipulate him; one she didn't particularly enjoy.

Craig Williams strolled into his opulent office and sat down in his over-stuffed chair; a nice gift from a grateful contractor. As he spun around to view the campus grounds beyond his office window, he put his briefcase on the side of the large oak desk and placed the manila folders Libby had given him on a matching oak credenza behind him. He looked around his office with pleasure and conceit.

At forty-two, he had achieved what most men only dreamed of— managing a multi-billion dollar space program, the most ambitious NASA program to date. What he'd had to do to get there didn't concern him at all. His only interest now was to stay on top and keep the funds, both public and private, pouring in. He was *almost* where he wanted to be and that was all that mattered. He dreamed of one day being appointed Director of NASA.

He glanced at the gold clock on his desktop. Another gift from a grateful contractor. His meeting with Michael Cason, Vice-President of Operations at the Parkin-Eldred Corporation, was in thirty minutes. He picked up the manila folders and again looked through them, this time with more scrutiny. He was ready.

Twenty minutes later the intercom light on his multi-net phone blinked. Craig pushed the button and asked, "Yes, Libby?"

"Your nine o'clock appointment, Mister Cason from the Parkin-Eldred Corporation, is here."

"Have him wait in the conference room. I'll be with him shortly. And Libby, be a good girl and make some coffee and put it in the conference room."

Libby bridled at the chauvinistic remark but Craig had already pushed the intercom button to break the connection before she could reply.

Craig leaned back in his chair and smirked. "I'll make the bastard wait," he said to himself. "I've got him by the short hairs and he knows it. I'll let him sweat a little."

Craig sat there alone in his office, the manila folders nestled in his lap. He spun his office chair around and around like a kid in a barber's shop.

As Craig Williams gloated behind his desk, Libby rose from hers and peeked into his office. She loathed the man with a passion, but she knew he was only one of the fish that would be fried. She hadn't succeeded in penetrating this deeply into the Hubble project just to blow her cover over some male chauvinist asshole.

She went out to the lobby, greeted Michael Cason, and showed him into the conference room. Then she went into a small room next to the meeting room, closed the door behind her, and started the coffee.

The coffee room was really more of a storage closet. Besides the usual office supplies, the room contained a large Brewmaster coffee urn. While the coffee was brewing, Libby carefully moved one of the file cabinets away from the wall. It was heavy but she was used to moving it. Behind the cabinet was an electrical outlet in the wall. Libby ran her hand down along the back of the file cabinet until she felt a small key taped to the metal. She pulled the key away from the cabinet and inserted it in the outlet. A tiny red LED light set into the cover plate blinked on. Libby checked her watch, it was 9:05. She pushed against the cabinet and it slid back against the wall. She returned to the Brewmaster and poured the steaming coffee into a small silver coffee pot. She then prepared a tray with cups and saucers and left the supply room, locking it behind her.

Craig Williams strolled into the conference room at 9:18 and sat in a chair at the opposite end of the table. He had a small stack of manila folders in his hand that he tossed onto the table towards his visitor.

"I don't like to be kept waiting, Williams. Who the hell do you think you are?" Michael Cason stormed. He stood at the end of the table, staring at Craig.

Craig Williams pretended not to notice the sudden outburst as he sat down. He began to peruse a document he had retrieved from the inside pocket of his suit coat.

"Sit down, Mike," Craig ordered in a soft but firm tone.

Michael Cason remained standing, puffing out sighs like a territorial confrontation between two animals.

"Sit down!" Craig shouted, this time as a command, and Mike Cason slumped into his seat like a beaten puppy. Craig pointed to the folders he had tossed on the table. Mike Cason picked them up and stacked them in front of him. He already had a pretty good idea what was in them.

"Unless you cooperate with me, Cason, the information in those folders in front of you will not only guarantee your unemployment, they will probably earn you at least twenty years in Leavenworth. Now am I making myself quite clear?"

Cason opened the top folder, looked at its contents with disdain and said, "Okay, Williams. You've made your point. Now what?" he asked, closing the file and pushing it away like a child who won't eat his vegetables.

Craig Williams pulled another sheet of paper from his inside coat pocket. It was identical to one that was already on the table in front of him. A broad smile came over his face as he slid the paper down the table to Cason. "Pick it up!" he commanded.

As Cason picked up the paper, Craig began to read it out loud. Cason followed along as Craig kept reading. He knew he was in too deep to walk away now. If word ever got out of what they were doing, it could topple the entire space program and take down Parkin-Eldred.

Above the center of the conference table, an air conditioning vent was suspended in the sculptured tile ceiling. Mounted behind the metal grill, a very sophisticated listening device recorded every word spoken in the room.

***

Hank Stanton pulled into his driveway, put the car in park, and turned off the ignition. He undid his seatbelt, leaned over to the passenger seat and retrieved the computer printouts. He sat there for a moment thinking about the events of the night before. He wondered what the symbols could mean. In the back of his mind he knew, but he would not consciously admit it to himself. Before leaving the lab he ran a multitude of diagnostic tests on the computer system to make sure it wasn't an electrical glitch or hardware anomaly that had caused these strange images he now held in his hands. As it turned out, the system was fine. Everything checked okay. Hank glanced at his watch. It was past nine and he was exhausted. He didn't really like working all night, but Craig Williams had him running a system interface with the Cartagay Island Receiving Station and…"Shit!" he exclaimed loudly. "If I received the symbols at Goddard, then McDaniels and Devane must have received them as well."

Hank looked at his watch again and did a quick calculation. Cartagay was exactly twelve hours behind the East Coast. It was after nine at night out there now. Hank breathed a sigh of relief. He was sure that McDaniels and Devane would spend considerable time attempting to decipher the symbols before reporting it to NASA. They probably wouldn't contact Williams until they had something concrete to tell him anyway.

Hank got out of the car and went into his house. He needed sleep, badly. His mind needed rest before he could return to the mystery of the symbols, and what, if anything, they all meant. Hank knew there was a lot to be done and probably not much time to do it.

Dropping his coat and the stack of computer papers on the closest chair, Hank went off into the bedroom. He went to the night stand where he had a small digital clock radio. He picked up the clock and set the alarm to go off at two o'clock. Just about five hours sleep, he thought. That should be enough.

He plopped down on the bed thinking somehow that the telescope was the key. A message from the Vega Star System. It's unbelievable, he thought.

As he fell asleep, the image of Libby Morales walking away from him flashed through his mind.

3

The planet Chulos is the fourth planet orbiting the blue/white star Vega, approximately 27 light years from Earth. The star had actually been discovered in 1983 by the Earth-orbiting Infrared Astronomical Satellite, though the image had been much too faint to see any planetary bodies that might be in orbit. Scientists had, at the time of its discovery, hinted that a solar system might exist there but without solid proof, astronomers directed their attention elsewhere.

Chulos was in a very large elliptical orbit around Vega, a star nearly ten times the mass of Earth's sun. The planet's distance was perfectly suited for the type of intelligent life that had evolved on it.

For the race of aliens that inhabited the fourth planet, the existence of Shoone Peltoran–3 (Earth) had been known for several million Earth years and Kamal Tarn, first Lector in the Circle of Comastyr, was the scientist (if such a term could be used) now responsible for observing the planet's development.

Direct interaction between his civilization and the people of Shoone Peltoran–3 was far in the future because the Peltorans were considered much too violent for personal contact, except of course for scientific research. But as Kamal had noted in the Council of Circles, that was already changing. The Chulosians were aware that another species had already begun to influence events on the planet, and something had happened that would soon lead to the total extinction of the inhabitants of Shoone Peltoran–3.

Their science and benevolence enabled the Chulosians to be the lifeform seeders of many planets in many galaxies. They could observe, communicate, and even travel to other planets in real time using a Chulosian device known as the Corbal Ring of Infinity. It was this device that Kamal Tarn was using to send his thought pictures through the Hubble telescope.

Probably the most amazing thing about Chulos is the planet itself. Unlike Earth, which has nearly two-thirds of its land mass submerged

under water, the entire Chulosian world is a brilliantly clear and spar-
kling ocean. The inhabitants of the planet live in this fantastic sea,
living, working, farming, and creating scientific marvels thousands of
years beyond the technology, and even perhaps the imagination, of
Earth people. The physical appearance of the water-dwelling Chulosians
could best be described as 'humanoid dolphin.'

Regardless of the depth of the ocean, there is no difference in the
pressure it exerts. The Chulosians can come and go freely at any depth
in total comfort. And although they can breath in the oxygen-rich
water of Chulos, they can also survive in an oxygen atmosphere for
extended periods.

Chulos sparkles like a glistening jewel in the Vega system. Its inhabitants have lived in peaceful coexistence with each other and their
environment for hundreds of thousands of years. The society of Chulos
is based on circles of knowledge and friendship. Each family of
Chulosians belongs to a circle, called a Chotor. It has been this way for
thousands of generations.

Like the spokes on a wheel, the family circles are all joined at the
center of their culture by The Circle of the Gee. Each Chotor is represented on The Circle of the Gee by a family member. The GEE is the
powerful and benevolent energy of light that pervades the entire universe, and the sophistication of Chulosian society and science rests on
their loving manipulation of the GEE.

The Chulosians have evolved far beyond what could be imagined
for Earth's own ocean living dolphins, yet there are some startling com-
parisons. The form of language on Chulos, although seldom used,
consists of a variety of clicks and whistles similar to the dolphins on
Earth. Their principle form of communication is called 'ring-talking'
or 'thought-merging.' It is the way they communicate their thoughts
and feelings. By forming water rings, they project the images in their
minds to others instead of speaking aloud in sentences. This makes
their language so much more colorful and descriptive. They have also
developed the ability of thought image projection and physical interstellar travel using a device called the Globe of Oreth that is placed
within the Corbal Ring of Infinity. By harnessing gravity waves, they
can project themselves anywhere in the known universe. They ride

these interstellar waves of gravity like cosmic surfers on some galactic sea. By projecting their thoughts to any point in space, they can travel instantly from planet to planet and system to system throughout the universe.

It was at the rim of the Corbal Ring that Kamal Tarn now stood, directing another gravity wave towards a distant planet. The Ring began pulsating as a holographic image of a vortex took shape in the center. Kamal guided the Cotera Tunnel vortex, a direct pathway from Chulos to the mirror in the scope. In an instant, the message he sent was received by some very puzzled scientists 27 light years distant.

4

Cartagay Island Station in the Pacific

Professor Devane looked up from the puzzling sheets of data received from the telescope and said to his colleague, "Brian, I think we should contact Goddard and inform them of this discovery."

"Edward, it's already past nine o'clock and I'm tired. Besides, do we really know what this discovery is? The transmissions stopped over six hours ago, and we haven't even begun to decipher what these symbols mean, if anything at all. You know as well as I that it could take days of painstaking analysis before we have a clue. I feel it would be more prudent for us to sleep on it and continue this discussion in the morning."

"But, Brian, this could be the discovery of the century and you act as if it's probably some equipment malfunction."

"And you, Edward, are beginning to sound like some first-year astronomy student who has just seen the rings of Saturn for the first time. We must employ scientific method here. We can't afford to be wrong."

"I suppose you're right, Brian, but what if the transmissions should begin again?"

"I have the system tracking the same astral coordinates. If anything should occur, it'll be recorded precisely the moment it happens. The station alarm will alert us if anything transpires."

Exhausted, the two scientists retired for the night.

***

On the planet Chulos, Kamal Tarn anxiously hoped the beings of Shoone Peltoran–3 receiving the message would be able to understand its meaning. He held onto the Earth images as long as he could before withdrawing them back into the Cotera Tunnel swirling in the center of the Corbal Ring. It was forbidden to defy the Circle of the Gee, but he felt compelled. Never before had the fate of an entire world been the responsibility of the Chulosians. Kamal Tarn knew of the disaster hurtling toward Shoone Peltoran–3. He had already stood within the Circle of Barsin-Gee and his own circle, the Chotor of Comastyr, trying to make them understand that as a benevolent culture, they must interfere. They remained adamant. The fate of Shoone Peltoran–3 is its own. The consequences of premature interference were too great to attempt even a thought picture transference.

Kamal understood their concern. The Chulosians had been to Earth many times and had interacted with selected humans by offering them the gift of the GEE. It had always ended in disaster. The few who accepted the wondrous gift of light were inevitably destroyed by their own people. Yet, through the generations, some still had the mark.

Kamal broke the link and the Cotera Tunnel was gone. He stood there, suspended in the watery matrix that was his world, and knew that he would have to try again. Soon.

***

Michael Cason left the building in a hurry. Libby was at her desk when Craig Williams returned from the conference room.

"How was your meeting with Mister Cason?" she asked.

"The usual. Manufacturing problems and production delays. It looks like I'll have to schedule a trip to Hartford, Connecticut tomorrow. Libby, would you make the travel arrangements? I'll be staying at the Sheraton. And Libby, have a car waiting for me at the airport."

Craig went into his office and closed the door behind him. Libby made some notes regarding his trip requirements on a legal pad and put it in her desk. She then got up and went down to the conference room to collect the cups and coffee server left from the meeting. Placing them on a small tray, she took them into the ladies room off the hallway and put them in the sink. As she stood there rinsing out the cups, she looked at herself in the mirror. She was a good looking woman. Most men desired her and rightly so.

Libby thought about Hank and hoped that he wouldn't somehow be drawn into all this intrigue and corruption. She liked him and had even had a fantasy or two involving the two of them. But Doctor Hank Stanton was absorbed in his work, and as far as Libby could see, that was all that mattered to him.

She thought of Craig Williams and his chauvinistic attempts at conquest. What a fool if he thought he would ever get to first base with her. Libby chuckled to herself as she stood over the sink; that jerk won't even get on the playing field. She gathered the rinsed cups and server from the sink and left the ladies room.

Libby looked nonchalantly around the corridor outside the ladies room to be sure no one was around. Seeing it empty, she unlocked the small supply room, entered, and locked the door behind her. She put the cups and tray down and again moved the file cabinet away from the wall. She inserted the key she had used previously, leaned down, and twisted the outlet cover that removed the device from the wall. Inside was a miniature tape recorder, not at all similar to a department store model. This was a highly sensitive piece of equipment, able to hear a pin drop in a crowded room.

Libby pressed a small button on the side of the unit and a clear plastic cover popped open to reveal a dual micro-cassette mechanism capable of recording two tapes, one after the other. She removed one of the tapes, took a blank tape from between her breasts, and slotted it into the tiny machine. She closed the cover and reinserted the device in the wall. She then removed the key and the red LED went out.

Satisfied that she had done everything correctly, Libby pushed the metal file cabinet back to its original position. The entire task took her less than three minutes. In five minutes she was back at her desk making reservations for Craig Williams, the retrieved cassette concealed safely between her breasts, to be listened to later that evening.

***

Go on, take the money and run, ooh-ooh-ooh. The alarm was set to music and the Steve Miller band was playing on the radio. Hank reached across the bed to hit the snooze button to turn off the music. He looked at the time: 2:00 p.m. He rolled over in the bed, got up, and went off to the bathroom to shower and shave. Hank finished in the bathroom and dressed, all the time thinking, "What does it all mean?"

He went into the living room and picked up the stack of papers he had brought home from the lab. In the kitchen, he tossed them on the table and made himself something to eat. As he ate, he spread the papers out on the kitchen counter. He noticed, as he did the night before, that the same symbol appeared over and over again. To him it looked like a dolphin with arms and legs. Instead of looking like some mammal at Sea World, it more closely resembled a humanoid in both stature and appearance. But even more puzzling was the halo of light around its head. It didn't make any sense, but something about these symbols nagged deep in his mind.

Hank looked up at the kitchen clock: 2:25.

***

"The captain has turned on the seat belt sign, sir. Please fasten your seat belt in preparation for landing," a flight attendant said. Michael Cason was sleeping in his first class seat when a flight attendant woke him. They were preparing to land the aircraft. "…tray tables and seat backs…" the announcement continued over the intercom.

He straightened his seat and moved his briefcase from the empty seat beside him to the floor under his feet. As he put the briefcase down, he thought of its contents and Craig Williams. Mike knew he was in over his head and that if the story ever got out he would be ruined. And that's looking at the bright side, he thought.

The plane landed and taxied to the gate. Mike sat there, looking out the window asking himself how he ever got into this mess.

Parkin-Eldred had won the contract to build the primary mirror assembly and other critical components for the Hubble Space Telescope. It was a monumental engineering task, one that had never been done before, nor could it have been done until now. New materials that had been developed within just the past three years were being used in the matrix of the mirrors. Also the technology used to grind the mirrors to the exacting tolerances required and the high tech laser interferometers to check their flatness had only recently been developed.

Mike Cason was going over the entire program in his mind as the plane taxied to the gate. Where did we go wrong? he asked himself. He knew the answer; his own greed and that of Craig Williams. Little by little, Williams had sucked him in, and before he noticed, Mike Cason was at the center of one of the biggest potential scandals in history.

When it was discovered that the project was going to lose a bundle of money, the plot was hatched to grind the mirrors incorrectly. It was Craig Williams who authored the entire plan. That's when the real conspiracy began.

To defraud the government and insure that the program would continue, Williams devised a plan that would force Congress to allocate more money for the COSTAR fix. As Craig Williams put it, "That's where the profit is. We just say it was a manufacturing glitch. We launch it and fix it in space." And so they sabotaged the Hubble telescope to keep the program alive and the contractor kickbacks rolling in for another three years.

Mike Cason, having only his briefcase as carry-on luggage, deplaned and left the airport immediately. He picked up his Jaguar from the short term parking lot and headed for his office. As he drove away, a gray rental sedan closed in three car lengths behind him. Mike was so preoccupied with the day's events that he didn't notice he was being followed.

5

The small town of Holden, Connecticut was about 18 miles from the Parkin-Eldred plant. It was a sleepy little village of about three thousand residents, most of whom worked at the plant. Mike Wooten had lived in Holden with his family for the past twelve years in a typical colonial house in a quiet residential neighborhood.

Three houses away from Mike Wooten's, on the opposite side of the street, Paul Gaynor sat in the rental car fingering the trigger on his Mac 10 Streetsweeper. The dull black weapon with the long padded silencer lay across his lap. Gaynor was like a cheetah: hungry, waiting for the moment to pounce on his unsuspecting prey. In fact, that's exactly how Paul Gaynor pictured himself. A creature invisible to his next kill. He picked up a pair of night vision binoculars from the center console and looked up at the house again. He had the patience of a deadly animal. The hunt was everything and he had been secretly watching and stalking Mike Wooten for nine days. Paul Gaynor was good at murder; he had been doing it for a very long time. In fact, he was regarded as one of the best hit men in the country. But Gaynor worked for only one man who leased him out to the highest bidder.

His present assignment was to cap Mike Wooten in order to send a message of fear to any others that might have the urge to blow the whistle. Not that Mike had; this was 'just a precaution,' as the client had put it. "Better to ward off trouble before it starts." Paul Gaynor could care less one way or the other. He just enjoyed the excitement of the hunt and the smell of the kill.

He glanced at his watch. He knew Mike Wooten's routine almost to the second. It was 7:35 p.m. and, like clockwork, the porch light went on at the Wooten house. This was too easy, Gaynor mused to himself. He stroked the metal stock of the weapon, caressing it like a lover.

"Have fun, dear," Carol Wooten said to her husband.

"I'll be home around eleven as usual, sweetheart," Mike Wooten replied, blowing a kiss to his wife as he stood in the doorway.

"You kids behave for your mother tonight, you hear?" he said affectionately to his children in the family room.

"We will, Dad. Hope you get an 'A' on your essay," his son called back.

Mike picked up his books from a small table by the entranceway and said good-bye to his wife again. He took his car keys from a hanging wall rack and went out to the driveway. He was taking a writing class at the local community college two nights a week. As he opened the door to his car and placed the books on the back seat, a gray sedan pulled across the driveway entrance, blocking any exit. Mike didn't notice the car until a voice called out to him.

"Hey, Mike. How's it goin'?"

Paul Gaynor was out of the rental car and standing at the foot of the driveway, the machine gun in his right hand hugging his side. It was already dark and the street was cast in long shadows. Except for the occasional porch light from a few of the surrounding houses, it was pitch black. Mike looked at the man beside the car blocking the driveway. The man was almost thirty feet away and Mike didn't recognize him.

"Can I help you?" Mike Wooten called out.

"I don't think so," Paul Gaynor answered.

The hit man raised the weapon and gripped it with both hands. At the same moment, Mike, already walking down the driveway, was close enough to notice something was wrong. But it was too late. A series of quiet whooshes sounded as a short burst of 9mm bullets left the silencer, ripping silently into Mike Wooten's body. He was thrown back against the open car door by the impact of bullet on bone and flesh. With a look of surprise and horror etched on his face, he slumped to the ground, the last gasps of air escaping from the gaping wounds in his chest. Gaynor, looking pleased with his handiwork, tossed the gun in the front seat of his car. He slid behind the wheel and before closing the door, took one more look at Mike Wooten's now lifeless body lying in a heap on the driveway, blood beginning to ooze down the slight incline. Gaynor put the car in drive and as he slowly pulled away, he murmured to himself, "One down, two to go."

***

Gaynor parked the car in front of his motel room, the Mac 10 now back in its case in the trunk. He picked up a small bag from the passenger seat, left the car and went into his room. Tossing his coat on the chair by the door, he sat down on the edge of the bed and began to dig into the meal he'd picked up at a fast food drive-through. He picked up the TV remote control from the night table with his free hand and flicked through the channels looking for a local news station.

After finishing the last of the French fries, he washed it down with a large gulp of soda. Satisfied, he reached for the phone and dialed a long distance number. Three rings later the connection was made. It was a recording. Gaynor listened to the four-second message. It was another telephone number. He hung up the phone and waited three minutes before he punched in the new number. This time there was a voice on the other end.

"How many shopping days to Christmas?" the voice asked.

"Two," was his only reply.

"Happy Holidays," the other voice said and the line went dead.

Paul put the telephone down and smiled. He looked back at the television. The news was on. He picked up the remote and increased the volume. The news anchor was reporting a breaking story of an apparent gangland drive-by slaying that had taken place a short while ago in the town of Holden. Paul snickered, "What's this country coming to? A man's not safe in his own driveway."

He picked up the remote like a weapon and pointed it at the television. "Bang! You're dead," he said to the woman on the screen and pressed the remote to turn off the set.

He pushed the button on the base of the night table lamp, turning it off. In the dark, he lay against the pillows going over in his head the plans for the next kill. He lived for the anticipation of stalking his victims, and how he would kill them. He slept like a baby.

Paul Gaynor, once a member of the elite Special Forces, had been trained as an assassin during the Vietnam conflict. He'd had only one superior, General Arthur Reynolds, now the head of a top secret military research laboratory in the California desert. Gaynor had been a captain under Reynolds' command during the war.

According to military records, Gaynor was killed in action and his remains were never found. He was now a killer for hire and was proud of his accomplishments. With 23 kills under his belt, he felt indestructible.

6

Hank Stanton pulled into Goddard Center at 3:20 p.m. He parked his car and headed for the lab. In his hand he carried a small leather briefcase containing the computer printouts from the night before. He had already determined where he would start figuring out this puzzle. But first he had to contact Cartagay to find out exactly what they knew, if anything. Fortunately, due to funding cutbacks, only three scientists worked on the current Hub monitoring project and two of them were out of town.

Hank walked into the lobby and up to the podium at the center of the large rotunda. A guard seated behind the modern security station was looking at a bank of closed circuit monitors when Hank approached him, holding up his ID.

"Good afternoon, Doctor Stanton," the guard said with a flourish.

Everyone at the Center treated Hank with polite and friendly courtesy. He was shyly amused by it. He considered himself to be just a simple scientist and nothing more. Ever since he was a child growing up in the suburbs of New York, he had been fascinated with mathematics and the stars. An only child of middle income parents, he seemed to excel in every academic program that he joined. A brilliant student, he was offered scholarships to the best universities in the country, eventually choosing Cornell in upstate New York, the home base of Doctor Carl Sagan, the brilliant astro-physicist and Hank's boyhood hero. After graduating with honors, Hank went on to earn his doctorate and then fulfilled his dream of working for NASA and getting accepted into the Astronaut Corps.

He was a handsome man of six foot one and kept himself in good shape by eating well and working out several times a week in his home gym. Dark brown hair, brown eyes, and muscular. At 36 years old he was in excellent physical and mental shape. But he wasn't much of a ladies' man, although you wouldn't know it to look at him. He was just too absorbed in his work to take the time. And that had cost him his marriage a few years ago.

"Good afternoon, Charlie. How's that family of yours?" Hank asked the guard sincerely.

"Alice and the kids are just fine, Doc. Thanks for asking. You workin' late again tonight?" he asked.

"Looks like another all nighter, Charlie. I've got a lot of research to catch up on. Could you do me a favor, please, and let the guard at the gate know I'll be staying late?"

"Sure thing, Doc. I'll call right now."

"Thanks, Charlie," Hank said, handing the guard his ID badge.

The guard slid the badge through a slot on the podium console. One of the monitors flashed Hank's name, department, and the time. A green light flashed entry approval and the guard handed Hank the badge. Due to the nature of the projects at Goddard Center, security was very tight.

Hank took the card and clipped it to his shirt collar. He waved to the guard and walked across the lobby to the door leading to his office and the Space Science lab. He punched a code on the door's keypad and a moment after it clicked open, he went in. It was 3:30 p.m.

***

Libby was in the middle of writing a letter on her word processor when the intercom buzzed. "Libby, would you come into my office for a minute?" What could he want now? she thought, rising from her desk.

A pile of manila folders were stacked on Craig's desk. The top folder had a one-inch wide red band around it with the words TOP SECRET in white letters. There was a knock at the office door out to the corridor.

"Come in," Craig said.

Hank Stanton walked in.

Libby heard Craig's voice and waited at the door that connected their two offices.

"Hank, it's you. What can I do for you?" he asked, trying to conceal the folders on his desk.

Hank pretended not to notice. He crossed the office to a chair next to a small cocktail table and sat down. He placed the leather case he was carrying on his lap. "Craig, what are Devane and McDaniels out at Cartagay working on right now?" he asked.

"Why do you ask, Hank? Is there a problem?" Craig asked, curiously. Most of the scientists at NASA, and especially Goddard, worked on their own projects. There was rarely any crossover of data unless the projects required it. Each team was pretty much in the dark about the other currently active programs.

Craig looked uneasy. He nonchalantly moved the manila folders to one side of the desk. He picked up some papers and placed them on top of the stack.

"Well, I'm not sure. I'd like to run a system-wide diagnostic test and it'll take us off-line for about five hours," Hank said.

"Didn't we just inspect the system a week ago? I thought the results of the inspection were okay. I can't afford to lose telemetry tracking for five minutes and you want to shut the system down for five hours. Are you crazy, Hank? Do you realize how important this research is to the Center? We're coming up for new appropriations in two months. If we don't show some results soon, we may just find our budget slashed. And that would wipe out your COSTAR mission. I need some good stuff for the PR people, if you catch my drift."

Hank really despised this weasel. Another bureaucrat, more worried about the money than the research, Hank thought, listening to Craig run on. He needed the lab time and the pretense of running the diagnostic. He wasn't ready to tell anyone about the strange transmission until he'd had a chance to analyze it himself. Besides, he hadn't spoken to the scientists at Cartagay yet and needed to know what they knew.

"Craig, I can only speak for myself, but if you think I or any of my colleagues would falsify data just to put on a show and save your ass, you're sorely mistaken." Hank was getting angry and a sharp edge was beginning to show in his voice.

"Look, Hank. I've had it up to here," said Craig, pointing to the top of his head. "We've got enough problems with the HST without you damned scientists screwing around with the system. I don't want any delays and that's final. Do we have an understanding? Because if not, I don't give a damn what *Newsweek* said about you. I'll see to it that you're back teaching high school science." Craig Williams was flushed and breathing heavily.

Hank stood up and walked to the front of the desk. "You pompous ass! All you can think about is your damned budget. If you'd have exercised stricter quality control measures when the HST program was underway we wouldn't be having these problems now. And don't threaten me, Craig. I'm not going anywhere. You know it and I know it." Hank turned and started toward the door to Libby's office when Craig called to him.

"I meant what I said, Stanton. Don't fuck with me!"

Hank opened the door to Libby's office and noticed Libby standing to one side. He stepped into her office and closed the door behind him.

"Did you catch any of that?" he asked.

"All of it. The guy's a total ass," she replied.

Hank was surprised at her response. He put his hand on her shoulder and whispered, "As big as they come."

Craig yelled into the intercom, "Libby, would you get in here. Now!"

Libby looked at Hank and said, "I'd better get in there before he has a cardiac arrest."

"Yeah. I almost wish he would. Save everyone a lot of headaches."

"See you later, Doctor Stanton," she said with a warm smile and went into Craig's office.

Cartagay Island

"Brian, please come in here and have a look at this will you? Oh, and Brian, please bring in page three also," Professor Devane called.

Devane was standing over a large light table, its white opaque acrylic top illuminated by large fluorescent tubes mounted directly under it. He was peering intently through a 30X magnifier at a transparent slide taken of the telescope's image of the Vega system. McDaniels was in the adjoining lab working on deciphering the symbols and rummaging through the pile of computer sheets he had spread out over the desk. He found page three and scooped it up.

"What have you got, Edward?" Brian asked.

"I'm not quite sure."

Taking the paper from McDaniels, Devane placed the computer printout on the light table. He then put the color transparency next to one of the images on the page and propped the magnifier over both of them. He looked intently from one to the other, back and forth, like someone watching a tennis match in slow motion. He looked down and then at his associate and then back at the table again. He finally lifted his head, scratched his temple, and smiled.

"Have a look, my friend."

Goddard Center

"Sit down, Libby. I have a few things I need to discuss with you," Craig Williams said, leaning against the front of his desk, his hands supporting his body on either side.

Libby sat down in the chair just vacated by Hank Stanton moments earlier. She noticed it was still warm; it excited her for an instant. Craig's eyes followed her movement in the chair, hoping for a glimpse of her panties. So predictable of him, she thought, crossing her legs and placing the pad she was carrying on her lap.

"Libby, I'm afraid we're having some trouble with Doctor Stanton," he said, moving away from the desk and standing in front of Libby.

She looked puzzled at Craig's comment about Hank. "What kind of trouble, Mister Williams? Nothing serious I hope?"

"Libby, what I am about to tell you must remain in strict confidence." He turned around and walked across the room. He picked up a chair, carried it over to just a few feet in front of Libby, and sat down. "Yesterday a Top Secret folder containing documents regarding the Hubble Space Telescope was taken from my office. These documents contain some very sensitive information. If they were to fall into the wrong hands, it could prove catastrophic for many people. As well as our government, of course."

Shit! Libby thought, almost saying it out loud. How could he have discovered that I took the HST file along with the other ones he gave me yesterday? The fool must have some other security system I don't know about. She sat there thinking, summoning up a false expression of shock. She couldn't believe that asshole suspected Hank Stanton of some kind of espionage. Hank was one of the most respected scientists in the country; he was even an astronaut. His loyalty was beyond reproach. Libby wondered if she might have underestimated Williams. Right now, she thought, he could be very dangerous.

"Mister Williams, even if Hank…I mean Doctor Stanton, did take them, isn't he cleared to view anything marked TOP SECRET? Besides, you couldn't possibly suspect Doctor Stanton of anything wrong. Why, all he thinks about is the HST project. He lives and breathes the Hubble," she said with almost a pleading tone in her voice.

"Libby, have you ever watched any James Bond movies?" he asked.

She nodded, a questioning look on her face.

"Well, he had this little trick to see if anyone had gone through his things. Now this is just our little secret," he said, as though they were conspirators. He leaned in a little closer to her, as if he were about to let her in on the secret of the century, and let his gaze wander down to her cleavage. Fortunately, the cassette tape was well hidden, Libby thought.

"I use a strand of hair," he said.

"A strand of hair?" she asked, pretending ignorance. "How?"

"I take a piece of my hair and lick it like this." He got up from his chair and walked over to the file cabinet and demonstrated the technique for her. "Then I place it across the space between the file drawer and the cabinet, like this. If anyone opens the drawer, the hair falls off. That's how I know he was in my cabinet."

"I don't mean any disrespect, sir, but how can you be sure it was Doctor Stanton and not someone else? For that matter, how do you know that the piece of hair didn't just fall off by itself?"

"I'm not absolutely sure. Not yet anyway, but I want you to keep your eye on the famous Doctor Stanton. I trust, Libby, that you will not mention this to anyone."

The phone in Libby's office rang. They both sat there as it rang again.

"Aren't you going to answer that?" he asked sharply, signaling that the meeting was over.

"Yes, of course. Excuse me, sir," she said, getting up and starting for the door.

"Libby, whoever it is, take a message. I'll be in conference for the next hour."

Libby walked out of Craig's office and closed the door behind her. She raced to her desk and picked up the call on the fifth ring. "Mister Williams' office. How may I help you?"

"Hello, hello." The voice sounded like the caller was on the Moon. "Ms. Morales, I think we have a bad connection. This is Doctor McDaniels at Cartagay Island. I need to speak with Mister Williams."

"Hello, Doctor McDaniels, I can hardly hear you. I'm sorry, but Mister Williams is in conference and can't be disturbed for another hour. Can I take a message and have him return your call as soon as possible?"

"Ah, please just ask him to call me as soon as he's free. Tell him it concerns HST transmissions."

"I'll do that, Doctor McDaniels, and I'm sure that he will call you as soon as he is through," she said.

"Thank you, Ms. Morales," he said, and broke the connection.

Libby grabbed her pad and jotted down the message, tore off the page, and got up from her desk. Walking over to the connecting door to Craig's office, she heard him talking loudly on the phone. She hadn't noticed any lights on her phone station so she figured he must be using the private line. She pressed her ear closer to the door. Craig sounded agitated and spoke quickly.

"I don't care. Just do whatever's necessary, but he's got to be the next target... Make it look like an accident... So change your plans and make it happen... Look, we don't have much time before he blows the whistle on all of us... Yes, he's that close... I don't want to hear from you until it's done... Do we have an understanding?... Fine. Good-bye."

Libby could only make out Craig's end of the conversation but it was enough to convince her that she had to act fast. She folded the message from Cartagay, went back to her desk, and put the folded paper in a small slotted message holder. She would give it to Craig later but right now she had more important things to do. She picked up the phone and dialed.

As Libby waited for the connection to be made, she sat at her desk and wondered if Hank Stanton was the next target that Williams was referring to. The phone was answered by a woman.

"Capitol Flowers. How may I help you?"

"Do you carry Flytraps?" Libby asked.

"Venus?" came the other voice.

"Yes. That's the one," Libby replied.

"What time would you like to pick them up?" the female voice asked.

"Five-thirty, please," Libby said and hung up. The meeting was set. She looked at her watch. Almost 4:30. She punched the intercom and asked Craig if he would be needing anything else. He said no and goodnight. Libby gathered up her things from her desk, switched off the desk lamp, and left for her meeting.

7

B rian McDaniels entered the Cartagay photo lab. "Edward, Craig Williams was in a conference so I couldn't get through to him. I left a message for him to call as soon as possible."

Edward Devane looked up from the pictures on the light table. "Brian, perhaps we're being a bit hasty in our analysis. I think we should give ourselves more time to evaluate this situation before revealing our hypothesis to Williams."

"Nonsense!" Brian exclaimed. "This is much too important a find not to reveal. At least our preliminary observations. I'm sure that once Williams understands the magnitude of this discovery, he'll want to engage the full resources at Goddard in researching this phenomenon."

"But, Brian, are we really sure what this is? We haven't spoken to Doctor Stanton yet. Perhaps he may have some insight as to what could have caused the scope to transmit these images. After all he is the team leader and it's our—"

Brian cut him off in mid-sentence. "Yes, yes. I understand that, but we have strict orders from Williams. Any unusual discoveries that can produce some good pictures will go a long way in the continuance of funding. Isn't that more important? Besides, Edward, I'm sure once we contact Mister Williams, Doctor Stanton will most definitely be brought into the analysis of this discovery."

Brian McDaniels just stood there. He looked at the pictures on the light table and wondered about the intelligence that sent them. Who were they? What did they want? What were they trying to say?

"Edward, this may very well be the most significant discovery in the history of all mankind. Should we just continue to sit on it and do nothing? Think of it. Possible contact with an alien civilization twenty-seven light years away. And in real time. It's absolutely incredible."

On the table was the entire complement of the 76 images received from the alien world. Brian leaned over the light table and pointed to the seven slides that were lined up in the center. Both scientists looked at them. Taken by the telescope with time lapsed photography, they were all the same; photos of a vortex appearing at the opening of the telescope's tube, and within the vortex there appeared to be an alien creature. It resembled a dolphin with arms and legs.

"Edward, it's almost seven in the morning and we've been at this for nearly an hour. What do you say we take a break, have breakfast, and discuss our course of action. By the time we're back in the lab, Williams will have called. I'm sure his input will have a profound effect on our next step."

"Yes, I agree," Edward said, putting the magnifier down. They left the lab, conversing all the way about the startling transmissions. The receiving station had its complement of technicians and associates but Devane and McDaniels were the only scientists in residence and the only people on the island monitoring the Hubble telescope. They thought it would be best to keep this discovery to themselves for the time being.

***

Karsal Cremboseedee was First Lector of the Circle of the Gee. It was the highest position of leadership and wisdom on Chulos. Karsal was part of the Chotor of Comastyr, and as such, was a close personal friend of Kamal Tarn.

All the inhabitants of Chulos belonged to one of the 26 circles that made up the Central Council that in turn formed the Circle of the Gee. The Chotor of Comastyr was an influential circle because it was the one that consisted of most of the practitioners of science. Kamal, as head of his Chotor, had taken the lead in the discovery of other shoones, or planets with intelligent life forms. Although their culture and beliefs prohibited them from direct interference with less advanced civilizations, they were sharing knowledge and wisdom with 17 comparable societies on other planets.

It was their position that Shoone Peltoran–3 would not warrant formal contact and exchange of knowledge and wisdom for at least 50 to 100 years. But that had to change due to the galactic catastrophe, the effects of which were already sweeping through the galaxy. Kamal

Tarn had discovered that a star in the Craytoll segment of space (the Guitar Nebula) had gone supernova. Kamal's research showed that this supernova was indeed different. The star was quite young and Kamal wasn't sure what could have triggered this catastrophe, but he had his suspicions.

Under normal circumstances, this event would be only a source of scientific curiosity for the Chulosians, and as long as it did not pose a threat to the shoones, it would for the most part be ignored. The Chulosians possessed the science and technology to protect their planet from any interstellar disasters that may occur, but Kamal Tarn knew that Peltoran–3 had no such protection. Nor did its inhabitants have the means to even detect such a catastrophe.

By Kamal Tarn's calculations, the exploding star had already emitted a radiation pulse that was hurtling through the galaxy at the speed of light, like ripples in a pond when a stone is dropped in it. The depletion of the ozone layer of Peltoran–3 had made it impossible for the intense radiation to be reflected off the atmosphere. The pulse's energy would boil the planet's molten core, causing it to explode. The result would be the total destruction of the planet and, of course, every living thing.

The only way for the inhabitants of Peltoran–3 to survive the impending disaster would be to replenish the protective layer around the planet by building a Pulsar Fence. This could only be accomplished through the exchange of knowledge from Chulos, yet this was strictly forbidden by the non-intervention policy of Chulos.

Kamal Tarn believed that if the Peltorans were to build a Crikodynke (Chulosian Pulsar Fence), it would provide the protection they would need to survive. It was this information and the plans for constructing the fence that he was projecting to Peltoran–3 in the form of images, albeit in defiance of the Circle's edict. He could not send any audio with the message because he knew that the Peltorans would not understand the language of the Chulosian people.

Kamal and the others of the Circle of Comastyr had watched and listened to the development of Peltoran–3 for many years. They could only project the language of another society by thought images and to do this they needed to be very close to the receiver of the thought-voice. Kamal knew that without a Focal Generator on or near the planet, no voice message could be sent or received.

Kamal Tarn had approached the Council and was given an audience within the Circle of the Gee. They were adamant in their stand of not interfering with civilizations of lesser intelligence. Karsal was the only Chulosian to support Kamal's position. Shooneenee Marfaldwyngee was adamantly against the proposal. He was ambitious and eager to pursue the exchange of knowledge and wisdom, but only with other intelligent worlds because of the opportunities for trade and the interchange of science and discovery.

The Chulosians had known for a long time that most of the civilized planets posed no threat to other inhabited planets. It was the inferior cultures that were barbaric and needed to be avoided. The Chulosians were not without experience in these matters. The incident on Melkos–3 would live forever in the memory of this peaceful and prosperous society.

The discovery of life on the third planet of the star Melkos had been exciting, for the planet contained many resources that could prove beneficial to Chulosian trade. The planet was almost completely covered by land. Only a few small areas of water were visible on its surface. They had studied the planet with the Craytoll Kooblund, an inverse image transfer device that could allow them, for short periods, to literally look in on another planet through a type of portal or magnifying lens. Their study seemed to indicate a quiet and benign society.

The Chulosians were also familiar with other civilizations in the parallel worlds. These were known to them as the Outer Rock Worlds, and one of them was already influencing the culture on Earth. And as Kamal knew, their presence wasn't always pleasant to the few humans who knew of their existence.

As far as the more advanced cultures inhabiting the outer rock-world civilizations were concerned, the inhabitants of Peltoran–3 were on the verge of a great awakening and were to be studied. Kamal wanted to provide the knowledge that might advance their evolution, yet he could not forget the tragedy of Melkos–3.

A circle of exploration had been organized and several Chulosians had been transported to Melkos–3. Their interaction with its inhabit-

ants resulted in them all being horribly slaughtered by a race of reptilian creatures that had masked from Chulosian probes their intelligence
and their ability to shape-change. Since the incident on Melkos–3,
Chulosian science dictated that an exhaustive telepathic wave link be
established in order to probe the minds of a planet's inhabitants. If
they were found to be hostile, then the only travel allowed would be
by holographic mass transfer image using the Corbal Ring.

This was the Council's current evaluation of Shoone Peltoran–3.
The inhabitants of the planet had degenerated into a race of hostile
beings and were not to be interacted with. The experiment by the
Chulosians that had taken place thousands of years ago in Peltoran–3's
past had been a failure.

Kamal argued that in many wave link experiments, he had discovered new emerging thought patterns among many of the Peltoran–3
inhabitants. Kamal's belief was that the genetic destiny with Chulos
that had been implanted in the DNA of Peltoran human ancestors
was finally about to awaken in them. Karsal agreed, but it was the
voice of Shooneenee that was the loudest, and he had swayed the ma-
jority of the planetary circles to support his stand against any contact
with the violent people of Peltoran–3. He believed that the ancient
experiment of marking certain human genes with the power of the
GEE had not worked and therefore they were to be left alone.

Kamal knew that by defying the Circle of the Gee and the Central
Council of Chulos, he could lose his standing in the Chotor of
Comastyr and be exiled from Chulos forever. As he stood before the
Corbal Ring, he thought of the consequences. If saving an entire planet
was within the science of the Chulosian people, then Kamal felt it was
their gift from the GEE to be sympathetic and lend assistance. He
tried to explain to the others that he could impart the knowledge without actually traveling there and thereby not violating the laws of the
Circle. They would not listen.

Kamal again stood before the Ring, about to repeat the message he
had sent before. And again, he defied the Council of Circles.

Hank Stanton sat in his office, a pile of reports on the desk in front of him. He flipped through the files until he came to the one titled *STS–38*, the analysis of the secret shuttle mission to the Hubble Space Telescope. Hank had suspected that a cover-up was being perpetrated in regard to the telescope's construction. He also thought that Craig Williams was somehow involved, but he couldn't prove it. Hank kept his suspicions to himself. Although he enjoyed some kind of celebrity status in the space program, and this made it easier for government grant acceptance, he was well aware that regardless of status, upsetting the apple cart could get him booted out. He knew that he had to be careful.

He turned to the images from the telescope. He had grouped them into four categories the night before and marked them in the order they were received. Several images seemed to repeat in each group. He concentrated on these first.

One group seemed to resemble some kind of amphibious creature. He wondered if such an evolutionary anomaly was possible. Another group of pictures seemed to resemble waves in a pond, each circle growing larger and larger as they spiraled away from the center. He reached into a file drawer in his desk and withdrew a folder marked *MKS–4327*. It was an analysis from the Mount Palomar research center of a star explosion that must have occurred a thousand years ago. He took out some of the printouts of the computer simulation of the supernova and studied them intently. "Yes, yes. There is a correlation here. I knew it!" he said to himself. He held up the page that contained the image from the Hubble and compared it with the simulation from Palomar. "Good God!" he said. "They're almost identical, but what the hell does it mean?"

Paging through the other papers, he tried to find some similarity. He couldn't. The other images were still just as perplexing as before. Hank picked each one up again, hoping that something would jog either his memory or his imagination. At this point, he didn't care. He glanced at his watch. Almost nine o'clock. He still hadn't called McDaniels or Devane. He pondered whether he should call them now or continue his analysis and wait until he had something a little more concrete to talk about.

He hadn't heard a word from Cartagay all day and figured that if they'd received the message, they surely would have been on the phone to Goddard. He was now a little more than just curious. Perhaps they had received the message but were trying to decipher it just like he was. He discounted this thought as preposterous. They were scientists. He was sure if they had anything they would call on a secure satlink from Cartagay.

Hank decided he would continue his own research until he either received another message, which he hoped would be transmitted again at 2:00 a.m., or made further progress as to their meaning. He decided that if he heard nothing from Cartagay by tomorrow, he would call them himself. He determined that no matter what, for the present he would keep this little scientific mystery to himself.

He had almost five hours to burn while he waited for a transmission that may or may not happen again. He decided that he would go into the lab at 1:00 a.m. Until then he wanted to do some computer sleuthing. Something else was nagging at him and he decided it was time to search for a few answers.

He turned his attention once again to the computer terminal on his desk and punched up the listing for the primary contractors on the telescope. He punched in another code and the printer turned on. A few moments later Hank had nine pages of data listing the name of every major company that constructed components for the Hubble telescope. The listing also cross referenced where he could find information on the sub-contractors that each of the 'primes' used. He began to make notes in the margins next to each company name.

Based on the findings of a secret shuttle mission, the suspected damage was indeed subtle. Torn brackets and mounting plates, the primary mirror askew. Those problems were attributed to the rigors of the launch and a failure to properly secure the internal components. The blame was placed squarely on the shoulders of the engineers and technicians at NASA. But those problems could never have happened during launch or any other time unless they were intentionally meant to happen. Hank thought this improbable. He wondered to himself, just as he had done since the discovery of the telescope's problems, why anyone would want to sabotage a piece of space hardware that could provide them with data for a decade of scientific research.

Pushing the printed list of contractor names aside, he punched up another code. A new file appeared on the screen entitled *STS–54*, the detail of the COSTAR mission to repair the telescope. He punched the same print code as before and the printer whirred into motion. As soon as it was finished, Hank picked up the printout and separated the sheets, placing them on the desk beside the other list.

Hank compared the two lists and as he did so, he made notes on the sides of each sheet. He sat there with both lists side by side on the desk in front of him. They were practically identical. Coincidence? He supposed that since these companies had constructed the telescope, it would be more than likely they would be involved in its repair. He felt that he had to go deeper if he was going to find the answers he was looking for.

Hank continued probing the computer's database. It couldn't be too well concealed since there wasn't any suspicion of wrongdoing; the answer was probably in plain sight, obvious but invisible to the casual onlooker. Hank noticed that almost all of the data he had been looking through had been entered or edited by someone with the initials E.M. He scratched his head for a moment trying to match the initials with someone at Goddard. Suddenly he exclaimed, "Libby!"

Hank wondered if she might be involved somehow. He hadn't forgotten yesterday morning. Libby was carrying a Top Secret folder in her shoulder bag. She was cleared for Top Secret data, as just about everyone at the Center was, but how often did employees take classified documents home? She should know that it was illegal to remove classified government documents from the lab. Craig Williams knew it too.

Despite the fact that Craig was an asshole, he was a stickler for doing things by the book. Why would he authorize Libby to take those documents home? Hank didn't want to be suspicious of Libby. He liked her and even toyed around with the idea of asking her out for dinner. He might do it now just to find out her level of involvement, if any. He hoped that he was mistaken, that it was just coincidence. He was tired this morning. Maybe he was wrong and it wasn't a Top Secret band on the folder. This amateur sleuthing was getting out of hand. If he kept this up, pretty soon he would be suspecting the janitor. Hank glanced at the folders and then at his watch. He still had a few more hours before he went to the lab.

He kept thinking about Libby. If she was involved with all of this and he let on that he knew, the first person she would contact would be Craig Williams. He was sure that Craig would attempt to have him reassigned in order to keep him from putting his nose where it didn't belong.

Hank sat there for almost an hour trying to figure out what to do. He was no detective and he knew from past experience that Craig was a ruthless administrator. Was he dangerous as well? The best thing to do would be to discreetly speak with Libby and find out exactly what was going on.

He looked at his watch again; almost 11 p.m. He suddenly felt hungry and realized he hadn't eaten a thing since before coming to the Center almost seven hours earlier. He didn't bring anything to eat and he didn't want to go out for food, so he decided on the next best thing: pizza. He ordered by phone and then called the guard gate to notify him to expect the delivery. While he waited, he continued scanning the images from the scope.

Thirty-five minutes later the phone rang in his office. He picked it up thinking it was the guard at the gate calling about the pizza delivery. It was Libby Morales.

"Hi, Doctor Stanton," she said. "The guard in the lobby said you were working late tonight. I couldn't sleep so I decided to come in and catch up on some typing I need for tomorrow morning. I just called to see if you might be needing anything. Maybe a cup of coffee or something."

"Thank you for thinking of me, Libby. I really appreciate it. And please stop calling me Doctor Stanton. You should know by now how I feel about titles around here."

"Sorry, Doct... I mean, Hank. I didn't disturb you did I?" she asked.

"No, Libby. Not at all. As a matter of fact, I've just ordered a pizza. It should be here any minute. I would be honored if you would join me."

Libby's face lit up at the invitation. "Thank you, Hank. I'd love to share your pizza with you. How about I come down to your office in about five minutes. I'll bring the sodas."

"Great, Libby. My other line is blinking. That's probably the pizza now. I'll meet the guy in the lobby and be back in two minutes."

"See you in a few minutes, Hank," Libby said and hung up the phone.

Hank punched the other button on his deskset. It was the guard at the main gate; the pizza delivery guy was on his way to the lobby. Hank hung up and called the guard in the lobby. He told him not to pilfer a slice until he got there and hung up.

Dinner with Libby, he thought. Hmmm. Hank liked the idea of being alone with her. Whenever he was around her, he felt a little tingle of desire, but usually he was too preoccupied to let it distract him. Maybe he might just ask her for a date. And maybe he could ask her about some of the things that had been nagging at him regarding the Hubble. He jumped up from the desk and headed for the lobby to pick up the pizza.

As he raced down the stairs to the lobby, Hank didn't notice Libby slipping into his office.

9

Phil Lombardo was shocked when he heard about the death of Mike Wooten. Why would anyone want to kill Mike? It had to be the Hubble and that bastard, Williams. He had been the one who had ordered the calibration error on the mirror. They were both paid to shut up about it and let management handle the situation, but Mike just couldn't leave it alone.

It was 1:30 in the morning. He sat there in the dark den, thinking. His wife, after three tries to get him to come to bed, was asleep upstairs. Phil stood up and walked over to the fireplace. He pushed lightly on the right side of the brickface. Several bricks were made of fiberglass and behind them was a small door. Built into the facade of the fireplace was a safe about eight inches square. He leaned down and dialed the combination.

Phil was glad he had the safe. He'd always told his wife that it was one of the best purchases they had ever made. It opened silently and Phil reached in and retrieved a brown clasp envelope with no writing or markings on it. Phil knew the contents like the back of his hand; his and Mike's insurance policy. Mike had insisted that he hold onto the envelope. Phil had wanted to make duplicates of the envelope's contents, but Mike insisted that it could be dangerous. He was going to suggest to Mike Wooten that he install a safe in his own house. Too late for that now.

He opened the clasp and unfolded the flap. He looked into the large envelope half expecting its contents to be gone. They were still there. He sat down in his Lay-Z-Boy recliner and pushed it so it would tilt slightly back. He sat there with the envelope resting on his chest for nearly an hour. He finally tilted upright and removed the contents of the envelope onto a small table next to the chair.

There were twelve photos in the package as well as several quality control documents and internal memos, all detailing the manufacturing and quality assurance errors in the manufacture of the Hubble telescope's primary mirror. The internal company memos, signed by Michael Cason himself, were probably the most incriminating evidence. They spelled out in detail the planned cover-up and deception to ship the defective mirror to the Jet Propulsion Laboratory in California. The company knew the Hubble would fail and already had plans to be involved in the repairs at three times the original cost. Phil thought the photos were just the icing on the cake.

He looked through the documents, making sure for the hundredth time that they were all in order, and placed them back in the envelope. He stood up, walked back to the safe and placed them inside. Leaving the safe open, he walked over to his desk, pulled out a single sheet of paper and began to write:

Dear Jenny,

If anything should happen to me like what happened to Mike Wooten, you are to give this envelope with its contents to the FBI immediately. You and the kids could be in danger. I just want you to know that Mike and I thought it best, at least for the time being, to keep quiet. I'm sorry for what we did and now the truth must be told. I love you and Dorothy and Phil Jr. I'm sorry I waited too long. I love you all.

Phil

He signed the letter and stapled it to the top of the brown envelope. He placed them back in the safe, closed the door, and spun the tumblers. He closed the brickface and went back to his chair.

Outside the den window, Paul Gaynor watched everything. What made him so good at his work was the fact that he really didn't have even an inkling of a conscience. There was not a single moral fiber in his body. He killed people for a living. It was just another job. Gaynor was an emotionless, instinctive, cold-blooded killer, primal to the point where he could stand outside a man's window in 30 degrees, his family sleeping in another part of the house, and murder him as easily as ordering lunch.

Paul had a modified Gloch 9mm automatic pistol snugged in his hand. Attached to the barrel was a six-inch custom silencer and laser scope. He really liked these weapons; he caressed them as he held them.

On cold nights like this, he thought it actually made the weapon perform better.

Paul Gaynor wasn't a very big man. He stood only five seven. Although he had been trained by the Special Forces in martial arts, he preferred the pistol, rifle, and machine gun as his weapons.

He crept closer to the window, careful not to get too close and have the condensation from his breath betray him outside. He saw Phil Lombardo close the safe and sit back in the chair. "Damn!" he cursed under his breath. He'd missed his chance because now the chair was blocking his shot and there was no window on the other side of the room.

Usually he was more precise. He was getting sloppy because this job was so damned easy. He couldn't let himself relax, not even for an instant. As if Phil had heard Gaynor's thoughts, he got up from the chair and went over to the television in the corner of the room. He could have used the remote but the *TV Guide* was on top of the console. He pulled the knob and the set came on, the volume blasting out at high level. He fumbled for the volume control and turned it down to a whisper.

Outside in the frost, Paul Gaynor almost jumped out of his skin at the startling noise of the TV. He watched Phil fumble with the set and as he did so he took aim for a shot through the glass.

Satisfied that the TV was now under control, Phil turned and started back for his recliner, not noticing the laser's red dot looking for its target. Without warning the glass in the study window shattered and Phil felt a terrible stinging sensation in his left shoulder. He instinctively touched his hand there and it came away wet with blood. Before he had time to think, five more shots came through the now broken window. Three of them slammed into his body. One went high and buried itself in the wall. The fifth hit the television, causing it to explode.

Phil slumped to the floor. He tried to grip the arm of the chair but the blood on the imitation leather caused him to slide off.

Paul Gaynor stood at the edge of the smashed window watching his quarry. Lombardo should be dead after so many shots at such close range, but Gaynor had to be sure.

Phil was still alive, moaning on the floor. Most of him was hidden by the chair, but Gaynor could see his head. He raised his gun for the kill shot when suddenly the whole world lit up. A woman standing in the doorway of the den let out a blood-curdling scream as the lights in the rest of the house went on. In a rush, Gaynor aimed and pulled the trigger. The shot went wide, missing Phil's head. The woman saw him clearly in the room lights and screamed again at the top of her voice.

Gaynor took off across the lawn, jumped into his car, and was gone.

***

The police and FBI descended on the Lombardo house like a swarm of locusts. Phil's wife was hysterical. She tried to explain to the FBI agents what she had seen, but she was borderline incoherent. In all the commotion, she completely forgot about the safe in the fireplace.

Phil was airlifted to New Haven hospital in extremely critical condition. Gaynor heard everything on a special emergency band radio provided by his employers. He hoped Lombardo would die. It would be his own demise if he tried to get close to Phil now. Well, shit happens, he thought. Only one doubtful hit out of 24. Not bad, he mused. No other hit man since Frank Nitti could make that boast.

Paul Gaynor checked out of his hotel and made arrangements to fly to Florida that evening. He wondered how the weather was in Daytona this time of year. He was confident it would be hot.

10

When Hank came back into his office, Libby was already seated in a chair waiting for him. He carried the hot pizza, shifting it from one hand to the other. He saw Libby and was caught off guard momentarily. He did not expect to see her in the office so quickly. He switched his gaze from Libby to his desk and the display on the computer screen. Had she seen it?

"Oh...er...hi, Libby. Geez, this pizza is hot," he said, still shifting it from hand to hand.

"Here, Hank, let me help you with that."

She took the box from him, and it *was* hot. She placed it on a small table against the wall. Libby had brought paper towels, plates, two cups and four cans of Coke. She opened the box of pizza as Hank came over to lend assistance.

"I can never figure out how these guys can keep this stuff so hot all the way from the pizza place," she said.

"Libby, this is the space age. Thermal pouches made out of new lightweight materials," he answered as Libby tore two pieces of pizza from the pie and placed them onto paper plates. He popped two of the sodas open, poured them into the cups, and handed one to Libby.

Looking at Libby in the subdued lighting of the lab, Hank thought she was very easy on the eye. She wore a pair of black stretch pants that looked like they might have been painted on, and a white lace blouse. Through the thin material of the blouse, Hank saw a provocative lace bra pushing her breasts up. She was tall, about five ten, but tonight she wore a pair of heels that added another three inches. Hank was taken with her beauty and stared at her a little more than was polite.

Libby was well aware of the effect she had on Hank. She was a beautiful woman who had been trained to use that beauty to her own advantage, only tonight wasn't the case. She really wanted to make an impression on Hank. He was a brilliant hunk with a good sense of humor. She was convinced he had nothing to do with the Hubble cover-up. Why not make a little play?

They ate in silence, looking at each other, smiling through the sauce and the cheese. Libby happened to glance over at Hank's desktop. She had gone through everything on the desk before he entered the office but if he had no involvement in this whole mess, why, she wondered, was he going through the list of contractors? I hope he isn't trying to play detective, she thought.

"How's your pizza, Libby?" Hank asked.

"Mmmmm, delicious, Hank. I didn't realize how hungry I was," she lied.

"Here, have another piece," he said as he opened the box. He took out a piece and put it on her plate.

As she took the plate from him, their hands touched briefly, sending a shiver down Libby's spine. She laughed to cover her nervousness. Did Hank feel it too? She felt like a schoolgirl finally getting noticed by the star quarterback.

They continued to eat their pizza in silence, smiling back and forth at each other like kids on a first date.

Libby began to gather up the cups and plates. Hank closed up the box and asked, "Want to take a slice home? There are three left."

"No thanks, Hank. I can't stand stale pizza. It would just end up in my freezer for a month until I finally threw it out."

They smiled at each other again.

"Hank, what are you working on that keeps you here at the lab so late every day?"

"Oh…I'm…ah…I'm working on translating some data from the telescope for Craig. He needs it for a presentation he's doing for the Appropriations Committee." Hank hoped she would buy into his explanation.

"Gee, Hank, it sounds real important. I'd better leave you to your work."

"Oh…ah…you don't have to leave yet do you, Libby?" he asked, surprised at how he could hardly form a complete sentence around this woman.

"Well, Doctor Stanton, do you happen to know the time? It's after midnight and I *am* a working girl. I have to be at my desk bright-eyed and bushy-tailed at eight-thirty in the morning."

"You're right, Libby. Excuse me. I really enjoy your company. Ah…perhaps…ah…maybe we could have dinner together sometime?"

Libby glanced at the pizza box he was holding and laughed. She enjoyed the effect she had on Hank.

"I mean a real dinner, Libby, in a restaurant." He tossed the box onto the table.

"I would love to, Doctor Stanton," Libby said, curtsying and smiling.

"Hey, that's great. How about next Tuesday after I get back from the Cape?"

"Gee, Hank. I don't know." She enjoyed how Hank brought out the coquettish side of her. Her lifestyle didn't give her much room to be playful.

"I'm leaving tomorrow for the Cape, Libby. I'll be there for about three days or so going over some of the details of the COSTAR mission. If you can't make it—"

She cut him off in mid-sentence. "Hank, I'd love to have dinner Tuesday evening. I'll leave you my phone number. Why don't you call me around seven and I'll give you directions."

Libby wanted to have dinner with Hank, but she also wanted to know more about his proposed absence from Goddard Center. Craig hadn't said a word about it. The hairs on the back of her neck began to prickle. Libby always felt that her sixth sense was a gift from her Puerto Rican ancestors. She was beginning to have feelings for him that went beyond professional, and her instincts told her that Hank could be a target.

11

Hank went to the Remote Telemetry Lab at 1:15 a.m. and made a preliminary inspection of the data recording equipment. He checked the telescope's present coordinates and sat back in his chair, waiting. Last night the signal was received at exactly 2:00 a.m. He checked the clock again: only 1:17.

On the computer desk in front of him he had spread out the print-outs from the last transmission. He continued to examine them and make notes in the margins. Still no contact from McDaniels and Devane out at Cartagay. Hank wondered whether they had received the data at all. They must have; every signal transmitted from the HST is received at both locations. He didn't think that they could have been running a diagnostic at the time. Besides, an alarm would have alerted them to an incoming signal. Then why hadn't they contacted Goddard?

He glanced back at the monitor and the digitized screen image of the Vega system, then down at the printouts. Suddenly something clicked and he pushed aside several sheets until he found the one he wanted. He picked up the paper and examined one of the images, a hieroglyphic symbol of two circles, one large and the other about a third smaller. They had what looked like streamers or rays of light emanating from the circumference. Around the larger circle were eight smaller circles and the fourth one had six wavy lines through it. The smaller circle had nine circles around it and the third circle had what appeared to be three wavy lines and three triangles within the circle.

As Hank examined the images he began to understand. He was looking at two planetary solar systems. Earth's solar system where humans are on the third planet, and the Vega system which apparently has some form of intelligent life on the fourth planet. Hank scratched his head and said, "That's incredible. Vega has eight orbiting planets."

"What's that, Doc?" a voice called out from the partially opened lab door.

Hank was momentarily startled and he spun around in his chair to see who was there. "Oh, hi, Leon. I didn't hear the door. I forgot that you're working nights."

Leon came into the lab pushing his Rubbermaid utility cart draped with cleaning utensils. He plopped his mop into a pail that was in a compartment underneath and strode over to the computer console where Hank was trying to cover up the computer printouts.

Leon Beardsley, a young African American of 21 had a passion for astronomy and an IQ of 175. His mother and father struggled to see him succeed, as did his five sisters and younger brother. They were a very proud family who believed in hard work. Leon was their hope and their future. He was the oldest child, and the first person in the Beardsley family to attend college. Enrolled at the University of Maryland, he was on a full scholarship and working at Goddard for the little bit of money they paid.

The real reason he worked there was for the wealth of on-the-job experience. Hank had taken Leon under his wing, and Leon had assisted him on several projects at the lab. The young man was a genius with computers and a whiz at anything to do with astronomy and the Hubble. He also had a keen sense of humor that was right out of the "'hood."

"Hi, Doc. I was just coming into the lab to dust around the counters and maybe damp mop the floor. I didn't know you were working late. Yeah, I'm doing the night thing so I can take in an extra class and spend more time at the lab. Whatcha got there, Doc?" Leon asked as he parked his cart in a corner and stepped behind Hank.

"Just some printouts from the HST, Leon. I'm working on a new diagnostic routine and I need to run it at night so it doesn't interfere with any of the experiments I'm running during the day."

Hank thought that was a pretty fair explanation. Leon was still a novice concerning most of the HST projects, but he hated to lie to the boy. Actually Hank liked Leon a lot.

Leon, who was very adept around computers, knew immediately that Hank was hiding something. One look at the computer screen told him it was in data pause mode while it waited for telemetry from the telescope. Leon had seen that screen a hundred times and knew a diagnostic mode from a receive mode. Leon was now really curious.

"Listen, Doc, I'm just about caught up with my duties for the night. How about I stick around and give you some assistance?"

"Thanks, Leon. This is pretty tedious work and I wouldn't want you to be bored," Hank lied.

"Me bored in this place? Are you kiddin' me, Doc? I could compile the mathematics of the ellipse of the Milky Way standing on my head and I'd enjoy it. Let me stay and help. Please," Leon pleaded. He'd never known Hank to refuse his assistance before. Whatever Hank was working on, it must be important to the Center and therefore the rest of the scientific world. He had to stay.

Hank would have loved to share this discovery with a bright student like Leon. He surmised, though, that with the current situation with Craig Williams, it would be best for Leon not to get involved. Hank was sure that as soon as word got out of this discovery, the government and military would clamp it down tighter than Fort Knox.

"I'm really sorry, Leon, but the project I'm currently working on is classified at a very high level." Hank hoped that this explanation would be enough to make the young man understand and leave the lab.

"Okay, Doctor Stanton, I can take a hint. Maybe I'll see you tomorrow," Leon said in a very formal tone as he wheeled his utility cart out of the lab.

"No hard feelings, Leon. This project *is* very important. Maybe I'll clue you in on some of the details tomorrow. Why don't you stop by the lab after your last class," Hank said, almost as an apology.

Leon stopped, turned and smiled. "Okay, Doc, that sounds great. I'll come around tomorrow. Four o'clock all right with you?"

"Yes, Leon, four o'clock is fine. Have a good night," he said as Leon left the room.

Leon pushed his cart down the hall, still curious about the project Hank was working on. He might as well keep himself busy and so he set off to clean the conference room and the offices in that part of the building. Wheeling his cart into the conference room, Leon looked around trying to decide where to start. He might as well begin with the big table, so he took a bottle of spray cleanser and began cleaning the fine wood surface. As he approached the center of the table, the air conditioner came on and a whiff of dust blew down from the vent.

Before he was done with the table, he should clean the ceiling vents. Nobody would want dust blowing into their coffee during a meeting.

Leon removed his sneakers in order to stand on the table without scratching the surface. He took his bottle of spray cleaner and a cloth and climbed onto the table. Spraying the metal vent grill with the cleaner, he began to wipe away the dust. He couldn't get at all of it, so he decided to loosen the two clips holding it up and swing it down on its hinges. He pulled it down to clean the other side and found Libby's hi-tech microphone taped to the inside of the duct.

He looked at the mike, trying to figure out why a microphone would be in the conference room duct in the first place. He stepped off the table and went over to his cart. In a side compartment was a little toolbox where he kept a small flashlight. He took it out and climbed back onto the table. He shined the light into the duct and noticed that the mike was attached to a small, powerful amplifier with a couple of wires leading away from it. He looked down into the room and realized that the duct went into the supply room next door. He jumped down from the conference table, grabbed his key chain from the side of the cart, and went out into the hall to the supply room.

He unlocked the door and turned on the light. The room had four rows of shelves that went from the floor to the ceiling. Boxes of paper were stacked on almost every shelf. There were two cabinets with twin doors that were the storage closets for stationary. A table with the coffee urn and a four-drawer file cabinet stood against one wall.

He looked closely at the file cabinet; there was something funny about the way it was placed in the room. He looked closer and realized that it wasn't exactly square with the wall. On the floor, he noticed a number of scratch marks in the tiles, as if the cabinet had been moved several times. Leon grabbed the cabinet on both sides and pulled it away from the wall. As he looked behind it, he found a key and noticed an odd-looking outlet with a key hole.

Leon studied the device in the wall closely, then inserted the key. He found that he could remove the unit from the wall and that it contained a small dual micro-cassette tape recorder. He took the tapes out of the unit and went back into the conference room. Inside a drawer in the cart were his school books from the day before and the micro-cassette recorder that he often used in class. He opened it and popped in one of the tapes. He turned the unit on and listened to the entire tape. Nothing. He took it out and popped in the second micro-cassette.

The second tape had nothing but static for almost twenty minutes and then Leon heard voices. He wasn't sure whose voices they were but he thought he recognized Ms. Morales as one of them. Wasn't she one of the only people allowed in the supply room? Now that he thought about it, she was always fussy about anyone going in there for anything. Even when he wanted to clean, she insisted that it was just a supply room and that it wasn't necessary. But why keep a supply closet locked? Leon's suspicions were running wild...what if she's a secret agent or...a spy? I better tell Doc Stanton about this right away, he thought.

Hurriedly climbing back on the table, he closed the vent. He then packed up his cart, put his sneakers back on, and rechecked the supply room to make sure that everything was the same as before. With the small micro-cassette tapes safely in his pocket, Leon raced down the corridor to the Telemetry lab. He glanced at his watch: 2:03.

***

Hank sat at the terminal, his eyes glued to the screen. Suddenly he jerked. Line after line of mathematical symbols and images scrolled on the screen. The system was already set to store and print each screen as the data was received so Hank just sat there, bewildered.

"Hey, Doc, what in the world have you got there?" Leon asked, as he came silently into the lab.

Hank was busy pulling computer paper from the tractor feed behind one of the printers and didn't hear Leon. A new series of images were being received from Chulos. Hank turned and realized that Leon was in the room. Instead of being angry, he just smiled and called to the young man to grab the paper feeding out of the printer as he went to the bank of monitors and punched several buttons on the console.

Leon tore the paper from the printer and looked at the monitor that was tracking the Hubble telescope. In the corner of the screen were the astronomical coordinates of the scope's target.

"Doc, could this be what I think it is?" he asked, a wide smile on his face.

"Leon, do me a favor? Lock the door and pull up a chair. I've got a few things I need to explain to you."

Hank now had an assistant.

12

Craig Williams arrived at Parkin-Eldred corporate headquarters at three in the afternoon, the same day that Hank and Leon received the new message from Chulos at Goddard Center. Craig was escorted immediately to Michael Cason's office. Mike Cason was seated behind his desk. Craig chose a well-padded sofa in the corner of the office.

"Would you like something to drink?" Mike asked, matter-of-factly.

"Yes, thank you," Craig said, almost too politely. He sat back on the sofa, relaxed and in control. He had already made up his mind how this meeting would go. It didn't matter anymore if Cason was in on this conspiracy or not. Craig had already determined that Cason, Vice-President of Operations of the prestigious Parkin-Eldred Corporation, was now a liability and had to be eliminated. He smiled wickedly and said, "I'll have a Coke, if it's no trouble."

"No trouble at all," Mike Cason said. He pushed a button on the intercom and asked his secretary to bring in a soda for his visitor. She came into the office a moment later with the drink in a glass filled with ice. Craig accepted the soda graciously and she left the two men alone in the office.

They sat looking at each other, Craig sipping his soda and Mike leafing through some papers on his desk. Mike was uneasy. Craig noticed it and felt more relaxed than before.

"Craig, I can't continue this charade." Mike blurted out. "I want out or I'm going to blow the whistle on the whole affair. I don't care what happens to me anymore. This has gone too far already. It's like a locomotive out of control." His feelings about the entire HST affair were more than he could handle.

Craig was convinced, now more than ever, that Michael Cason had to be eliminated. He just sat there, sipping his soda like some sadistic Roman governor about to turn his thumb down at a wounded gladiator. He looked up at his adversary and placed the glass of soda down on the table in front of him. He stood up and walked to the edge of the desk. "Mike, Mike, take it easy. I understand exactly how you feel. You have a large company to run here. I have every intention of letting you off the hook. But first I need some assurances."

"Assurances?" Mike asked. "What kind of assurances can I give you, other than I won't blow the whistle on the whole damn scheme and get us all thrown into Leavenworth. I'll give you assurances all right. Just remember, Craig, I documented every transaction we've made. Let's call it insurance to keep the partners honest."

"Mike, I don't care if you've taped every word we've ever spoken. I told you the truth. If you want to be taken off the hook, consider it done. I won't approach you on the subject again. You and your company will be treated like every other contractor. Your bid for new contracts will be grouped with all the others. No preferential treatment. But remember, though, I can't make any guarantees that you'll be awarded any contracts in the future. Consider it a quality assurance issue."

Mike Cason stood up from behind the desk and pointed his finger in Craig's face. "Get out of my office, you slime! I curse the day I ever did business with you."

"I'm sorry you feel that way, Mike. We could have made billions together," Craig said, walking back over to the sofa and picking up his briefcase.

He turned to say good-bye to Mike Cason, but Mike had stepped out from behind his desk and was right behind Williams. Cason was a big man. A retired Air Force colonel, he had joined Parkin-Eldred after leaving the service almost 15 years ago.

"Craig, I know about Wooten and Lombardo. I can't prove that you had anything to do with what happened to either of them, but I'm sure the FBI would be very interested in what I might have to say. So don't get any ideas."

"Don't threaten me, Mike, it doesn't suit you. You won't be hearing from me again. And don't worry, I wouldn't lay a finger on you," Craig finished his sentence and with briefcase in hand, left Cason's office.

Once outside he got in his rental car and headed back to the airport. He dropped the car off at the rental company lot and took the shuttle bus to the terminal. Libby had booked him an open-ended round trip ticket to Washington's National Airport, but Craig wasn't flying back to Maryland tonight. He got off the shuttle bus at the Delta terminal and purchased a one way ticket to Orlando for 8:00 p.m. He looked at his watch; he had two hours to kill.

The plane landed at Orlando International Airport at 10:35 p.m. Craig carried only his briefcase so he went right to the Alamo shuttle bus to get a ride to his rental car. Once he had the car, he set off for Interstate 4, an hour's drive to Daytona Beach. He had made a reservation at the Daytona Beach Marriot, where Paul Gaynor would meet him at midnight.

Craig arrived at the hotel at 11:50, dropped off his car with the valet, and checked in. Paul Gaynor was checked in under the name of Dave Smith. Craig went to a house phone and dialed the hitman's room. They arranged to meet in the patio bar in five minutes. Craig hung up the phone and walked through the lobby to the poolside bar. It was hot and humid for a September evening. He sat at an empty table and ordered a soda from the waitress. Two minutes later, Paul Gaynor walked through the patio doors.

"How was the flight?" Paul asked, sitting down in the chair opposite Craig's.

"Fine. I'm leaving in the morning for Goddard. As I told you on the phone, we have to make a slight change in our plans."

"What do you consider a slight change?" Gaynor asked.

"As it turns out, I was right about Mike Cason. He's far more dangerous to our plans than I had anticipated. He has to be silenced before he can speak to the FBI."

The waitress came over with his drink and asked Gaynor if he wanted anything. Paul ordered a draft beer in a chilled glass. The waitress left and they continued their conversation.

"Do you really think that he'd be stupid enough to go to the Feds?" Gaynor asked. "They'd put him in the slammer quicker than you could blink."

"He's getting jumpy. The murder of Wooten and the botched attempt on Lombardo have made—"

"Hey, I told you what happened with Lombardo. I had him cold. If only his stupid wife hadn't shown up when she did, he'd be dead as a door nail."

"You should have killed them both," Craig said.

"Hey, I only had seconds to get out of there. If I'd stayed any longer we all might be sitting in the slammer right now. Besides, his wife wasn't in my contract."

"It doesn't matter. Lombardo is in a coma and probably won't make it anyway. Cason is more of a liability now. I don't care how you do it, just make sure it looks like an accident. No screw-ups this time. We can't afford to let him live," Craig said. He was beginning to feel uneasy around the hit man. Even being seen with him could upset his own plans, he thought.

"What about the other items on the shopping list?" Gaynor asked.

"After Cason, you'll receive new instructions in the usual manner. We may have to wait a few weeks until the next target can be disposed of. I have other considerations now that must be addressed first."

"Is there anything else?" Gaynor asked.

"No. I think that pretty much covers the present situation. When will you be traveling back to Connecticut?"

"Soon," the hit man said, getting up from the table. "I think I'll take a walk on the beach. I love the smell of the ocean. Don't you like the ocean? The smell, the sound of the waves crashing on the shoreline. Guess not, huh?" He took one last pull on his beer, set the glass down and walked away from the table without saying another word.

Craig watched him walk across the patio and down the stairs to the boardwalk that paralleled the beach. The man was a cold-blooded killer, he thought. There was something different, strange about Gaynor. It bothered him that Gaynor was so nonchalant about murdering people in cold blood. Craig actually thought the guy enjoyed it. Well, I suppose that's why the General recommended him.

The waitress returned to the table and broke his train of thought. Craig ordered another drink, this time one with alcohol in it. The waitress returned with his drink and Craig sat alone in the patio bar, thinking about how he developed the Hubble scheme in the first place.

It had begun over three years ago when he was a program manager of a low-level NASA project at China Lake Naval Weapons Center in California working on a joint project with the Navy. An atomic clock to be used in the new Carter class of nuclear attack submarines required that he travel often to the Goddard Space Flight Center, where the Navy had a perfectly calibrated cesium clock that was the standard for the subs.

Craig already knew about the Hubble project, a popular but troublesome program at the space agency. Everyone was aware of the mounting cost overruns and delays with contractors. Quite a few people believed the project to be doomed from the start. Only a handful of congressmen supported it, but as everyone in Washington knew, it was the President's baby. In fact, the President felt as strongly about the Hubble as Kennedy had for landing men on the moon. The President was often quoted as saying publicly how critical the Hubble was in maintaining America's technological lead in space.

Craig thought about the way he maneuvered himself into the position of program manager of the Hubble project. He accelerated the development of the sub clocks by making deals with contractors, assuring them of continued work with NASA. The contractors were very pleased with this arrangement and showed their appreciation by finishing the project under budget and on time. They also kicked back nearly $200,000 to Williams. He liked that arrangement too, and so the NASA kickback conspiracy was born.

Craig thought that if he could get some of the same contractors on the Hubble project, he would get rich beyond his dreams. There would be enough government work to keep them busy into the next century.

Craig secretly worked out a plan with several of the contractors to intentionally overcharge NASA for the Hubble components. Since they had already started on the program, there was no way the funding would be reduced. And of course, if some of the components failed immediately after launch or soon after in space, he would be required to develop and head up any repair project. The contractors would have years of work ahead of them.

The one element he couldn't control was Lt. General Arthur Reynolds, the commanding officer of a top secret lab at China Lake, known to a few as The Mine. Craig was vaguely aware of it, but General Reynolds was very guarded. Anyway, Craig didn't care. He kicked back the General's share on a regular basis and that seemed to keep him happy. What Craig didn't know was that General Reynolds also had a lot of secrets and much more to hide from people in higher places than Craig Williams.

The additional thorn in Craig's side was Dr. Hank Stanton. Craig knew that Stanton suspected something. It was Stanton who got NASA to approve the secret inspection mission that discovered all of the problems with the scope. And it was Stanton who developed the COSTAR mission in order to repair the telescope's eyesight.

Craig grew more and more angry as he sat there remembering the past. He should have dealt with Hank Stanton from the very beginning. He had waited too long. Well maybe not.

He looked down on the beach. The bright lights of the hotel lit up the sand and the waves as they broke on the shore. He saw Gaynor standing at the edge of the breakers, throwing something into the water. The waitress returned and told him it was last call. Craig looked at his watch, it was almost one o'clock in the morning. He had a 7:30 a.m. flight to Washington National.

He threw a twenty dollar bill on the table and left for his room. As he walked back to the hotel, Craig turned to look at Paul Gaynor one more time. A shudder went through him.

***

As Craig Williams' plane made its final approach into Washington National, Paul Gaynor was changing planes in Atlanta. The hit man carried only a small overnight bag; his weapons were already in Connecticut and he had only to retrieve them from a U-Stor-It warehouse. He had weapon caches stashed in several locations around the country, usually within a few hours drive from his target. It was more convenient that way, and much less risky.

Those who knew Gaynor called him 'The Viper.' His bite was always deadly. He had earned his notoriety by killing a number of well-placed and uncooperative businessmen. Always successful in his assignments, he was particularly brutal in the way he carried them out. As a result of his success, he was hired by General Arthur Reynolds on many occasions.

Gaynor arrived in Connecticut at 3:00 p.m. He picked up the rental car with one of his many phony IDs and drove to the vicinity of the Parkin-Eldred plant, already knowing his victim's routine. Gaynor had already developed quite a file on Mike Cason but wanted to spend a day following him around just to be sure. He waited in the visitor lot, watching for Cason to leave. It was almost eight o'clock when he saw Cason get into his blue Jaguar. Nice car, Gaynor thought. Shame to have to ruin the paint job.

He followed Cason all the way home, carefully staying inconspicuous. Cason lived in a posh, sparsely populated suburb in Connecticut in a mansion on a beautiful fifteen-acre plot. Gaynor was satisfied that Cason took the same route home every day.

The next day, at the top of a steep rise, a bullet blew out the front passenger tire on Cason's Jaguar. The car skidded around a very sharp bend in the road, spun out of control, and went down a steep embankment. Gaynor removed a small silver box from his coat pocket. As the Jag rolled down the embankment, Gaynor pressed a black button on the box. The Jag exploded in flames as it continued down the steep hill.

The small incendiary device in the Jag's gas tank was almost impossible to trace, but so effective, Gaynor thought with deep satisfaction. With a broad smile, he watched as the fire ball hurtled to the bottom of the steep ravine, the intense heat scorching the flesh off the occupant's bones.

Satisfied that he had accomplished his task, he put the rental car in gear and drove back to his motel. Still two shopping days to Christmas.

13

Hank and Leon worked in the space science lab until five in the morning. Hank noticed that some of the images received this time were different from the previous ones. He also noticed that the last transmission seemed to stop right in the middle of an image. Hank compared it to a phone line being cut. Still, the number of symbols in this transmission exceeded the previous one by almost a third.

Leon, although he lacked a lot of practical experience, had one hell of an imagination. He was able to decipher many of the symbols using a mathematical code he was playing around with. It involved the interpolation of linear graphic symbols and a CAD system post-processor that converted lines into numbers and then back into lines again, forming an image. These were then cross-referenced with an ILM/SGI 3310 graphics database that matched the lines and symbols with known mathematical objects. Hank thought the results were astounding. If Leon was correct in his interpretation, the Earth was most certainly directly in the path of a blast of interstellar radiation that, without the protection of the ozone layer, would most certainly destroy all life on the planet.

"Well, Doc, I really think we should have someone double-check these findings," Leon said, weary from staring at a computer screen for over three hours.

" I have to leave for the Cape in eight hours. If I don't get some sleep I'm going to collapse. There's several things I need you to do for me. Write this down," Hank said. "First, everything that has taken place here tonight is to remain confidential until we can get solid confirmation on our findings. Second, I want you to have Libby Morales contact McDaniels and—"

"Geez, Doc," Leon interrupted, "I almost forgot in all the confusion. I found this tonight when I was cleaning up in the conference room. It was actually in the supply room next door," as he pulled the micro-cassette recorder out of his pocket. "There's a hidden microphone for recording conversations in the conference room air duct and a tape recorder mounted in the wall of the supply closet. What do you think it means? Libby Morales is practically the only person who uses that room." Leon handed the small tape recorder to Hank.

Hank looked at the small device for a moment and then turned it on. Craig Williams was talking with another person Hank didn't know. Libby's voice was on it also, but only in the very beginning. From the tone of the conversation, Hank surmised that Craig Williams was up to his neck in shit. Leon looked totally confused by the whole thing.

"Leon, I want you to make a copy of this and then put it back where you found it. Do it as soon as you leave the lab. It might be interesting to find out who retrieves this little beauty."

Hank handed the small recorder back to Leon. "Now back to what I was saying. Have Libby call McDaniels and Devane and tell them to contact me at the Cape as soon as possible. Here's the number where they can reach me." He jotted a number down on a small piece of paper and gave it to Leon. "I also want you to take a copy of these printouts and keep working on them. If they mean what I think they do, then this planet of ours is receiving one helluva wake up call from some extra-terrestrial neighbors."

"Geez, Doc. This stuff is blowin' my mind," Leon said.

"Pay attention. Keep a copy of that number with you and as soon as you have anything else—I don't care how ridiculous—you call me at the Cape. I'm going to try and finish up this briefing as quickly as possible so I can get back to Goddard."

"You know, Doc, sooner or later we're gonna have to tell someone about this. I mean, somebody way up there, like maybe even the President."

Hank didn't answer. He knew that Leon was right, but he had to buy some time and sort things out. He got up from the chair and grabbed the computer printouts from the desktop. He loaded the papers into a photocopier.

"Doc, this whole thing has me a little frightened and very confused. Shouldn't we be telling the other scientists here at Goddard about this? At least we *have* to tell Craig Williams, er, don't we, Doc?" Leon asked.

"Not yet, Leon. This discovery is too important. We can't let this information fall into the wrong hands."

Hank saw that Leon was agitated about all the subterfuge. He had to make him feel at ease or this whole situation could be yanked right out of their hands. Hank realized that they were experiencing a significant moment in the history of science, but he had to wait until all the facts could be collected and analyzed. Hank's real fear was that the military would step in and all the information they had interpreted so far would be locked away somewhere and labeled Top Secret. Hank kept thinking about the aftermath of Roswell. It had happened before and he couldn't afford to let that happen again. His biggest worry right now were the two scientists at Cartagay. He had to find out if they knew what was happening.

They packed up all the documents and left the lab. It was six-thirty in the morning.

***

Hank arrived at Kennedy Space Center that evening. He stayed at a small motel on Cocoa Beach while he attended briefings on the COSTAR mission at the cape. As soon as he checked into the motel, he placed a call to Leon. "Have you been able to come up with anything more on the transmissions?" he asked.

"Yeah, Doc. This is amazing stuff. It looks like the images are being broadcast from the fourth planet orbiting Vega. The closest thing the computer can make out for a name is something that sounds like 'Chulos.' The people there, if you can call them people, all seem to be related to Flipper."

"Related to who?"

"Flipper. You remember, that show about a dolphin that lived in the Florida Keys. These Chulosians are some kind of intelligent dolphins, or something real close to that."

"Leon, that's marvelous! This has to be the most amazing discovery in the history of mankind!" Hank said excitedly.

"That's not the half of it, Doc. There's a lot more to the message they seem to be trying to send us. There's also some kind of instructions or blueprint for some kind of tower array or something. I still haven't figured that one out yet. Have you contacted those guys at Cartagay yet? I told Libby and she said they called Craig Williams the other day but he was too busy to talk to them. She still hasn't been able to give him the message and I think he's out of town until tomorrow. Does that buy us some time, Doc?"

"I don't know, Leon. I'm going to try and get through on a secure satlink hook-up direct to Cartagay. You stay on it and I'll be back at Goddard as soon as I can."

"Okay, Doc. Keep in touch. Bye."

Hank disconnected the call and then redialed the number for the direct Satlink hook-up to Cartagay Receiving Station. McDaniels picked up on the seventh ring.

"Hello, this is Doctor McDaniels."

"Hello, Brian. This is Hank, Hank Stanton. How are you?"

"Doctor Stanton, Hank. How good to hear from you. We've been trying to get through to Goddard for the past three days. Where is everyone, on vacation?"

"Everyone's busy I guess. How is Edward coming along?" Hank asked, getting impatient with all of the hellos and how are you doings. He wanted to know if they had anything on the Hubble transmissions.

"Edward is fine. All is well out here in this remote paradise. Hank, something very strange has been happening out here. We were hoping you might be able to shed some light," Brian said.

Edward came into the room and stood next to him, trying to listen in on the conversation.

"Hank, Edward just stepped in. Would you mind if I put us on the speaker phone?"

"Please do, Brian," Hank said.

McDaniels pushed a small button on the telephone base and replaced the handset back in its cradle. The speaker came on.

"Hello, Doctor Stanton. This is Edward Devane. How are you?" he asked.

"Fine, Edward, I'm just fine. Now please, tell me, what's going on out there?"

"Well, we have been receiving some strange transmissions from the telescope. We know that it's not an equipment malfunction. We ran an exhaustive diagnostic test and everything checked out perfectly. Are you familiar with the scope's current coordinates, Doctor Stanton?"

Hank had to tell them. They were scientists, and very good ones at that. They needed to share their information.

"Brian, several days ago I received a transmission that came through the telescope from a planet approximately 27 light years away. It's the fourth planet orbiting the star Vega. The transmission was in the form of images and what appears to be mathematical symbols of some kind. We have been able to decipher a small portion of the message but there's still a myriad of things we don't understand," Hank said. He didn't want to reveal too much until he was sure that the two scientists and himself were on the same team and could cooperate fully.

"Yes, yes, Doctor Stanton. We've received the same messages out here at Cartagay Island. Edward and I have made significant progress in figuring out their pictographic system of symbols and images. We think that the first message was some kind of warning. The second transmission repeated the first one in that we again received the same warning. Only the second transmission contained a portion of a blueprint for building some kind of atmospheric molecular exciter, a phased-array that we believe will re-energize the Earth's protective ozone layer. The second transmission seemed to be cut off in mid-sentence. We don't know what to make of it."

Hank was excited at hearing about the progress the two scientists had made in so short a time. He sat on his motel room bed, thinking furiously. Outside, the usual Florida afternoon thunderstorm unleashed torrents of rain that pounded on the roof of the motel. Hank went on to relate Leon's breakthrough to the two scientists. Brian and Edward were amazed at the discovery of a new intelligent species that Leon had named 'Chulosian.' The dilemma they faced now was quite simple, he thought: What do they do with this information?

"Gentlemen, now that we have progressed to this point, where do we go from here? There's still a portion of the transmission we haven't deciphered. Could it hold other more important discoveries? And what about this thing that resembles a pulse of radiation racing through the galaxy? When will it reach Earth, and what will we do when it does?"

The questions poured out of Hank as he anguished over what they should do next. How could they possibly keep this a secret? But who could they trust?

14

Craig Williams arrived back in Maryland and went home and then to his office. It was late in the evening and he had to pick up some papers he needed for a meeting with several contractors in California the following day. His flight out was scheduled for 6:00 a.m. As he arrived at Goddard Center, he was surprised to find the young black janitor in the Remote Telemetry Lab.

"What the hell are you are doing in a restricted area, and at this time of night?" Craig demanded, as he stood in the doorway. He'd seen the janitor around the Center if he'd been working late and knew he was called Leo or something like that.

Leon was busy keying codes into the computer. He was running one of his own programs that cross-checked the data from the Hub. Leon knew he had to think fast or Mr. Williams would have his ass.

"Uh…hi there, Mr. Williams. Uh…yeah…I'm…uh working on some formulas for Doctor Stanton. I have his permission to work in the lab. I am a graduate student, sir, and I'm quite capable of handling this equipment. No need to worry, sir," Leon answered nervously.

"I'm not the one who should be worried. Do you know that this is very expensive and sensitive equipment? The work we do here is classified. I suppose Doctor Stanton failed to mention that little item." Craig was visibly fuming.

"I'm sorry, Mister Williams. I didn't mean any harm. I'll just pack up my stuff and be outta here. Tonight is my regular night off but I figured I'd help the Doc out by doing some number crunching for him," Leon said. He began to gather up the computer printouts he was translating when Craig walked over and slammed his hand down on the pile of papers.

"I think it would be best if you left these documents here, young man," Craig said.

"But, Mister Williams, I was working on those computer files for Doctor Stanton. He would want me to finish them," Leon pleaded.

"Let me be responsible for that. I'll see to it that Doctor Stanton understands the severity of this situation. Now goodnight, Leo. And if I catch you in this or any other unauthorized location at the Center again, you just might find yourself unemployed. Do you understand?"

Craig sounded like a pompous plantation owner chastising a wayward slave. Leon felt like decking him right there but he held his temper in check, got up from the desk, said goodnight, and left.

He immediately drove home and called Hank in Florida. He wasn't in his room so Leon left a message for him on the motel's voice mail system. He was worried that Craig Williams would go through the papers and find out what they were up to. He was glad for one thing, though. At least he had copies of every sheet at home.

Craig sat down in the chair vacated by Leon and started leafing through the papers that were still on the desktop. He couldn't make head or tails out of most of it, but one thing he did know: they were definitely Hubble transmissions. He gathered them up and took them to his office and then stuffed them into his briefcase. He would look them over more carefully on the flight to LA the next morning. Maybe this—whatever it was—would provide him with some bargaining power with General Reynolds.

***

Hank had been in meetings and training sessions all day with Mark Ramius and Bill Heller, the other astronauts who would be assisting him on the COSTAR mission. There would be two other astronauts on the mission but they would be involved with other tasks. They had been busy training in the weightless environment training facility pool, similar to the one in Houston, testing the effectiveness of the new Manned Maneuvering Units and the Safer jetpacks.

It was monotonous and tiring work, repeating the same test and movements, time after time after time until it became instinct. Although Hank was anxious to get back to Goddard and continue his research, he wasn't about to jeopardize the mission by getting sloppy with training. Their lives depended on one another; nobody wanted to be the first astronaut lost in space.

Hank got the message as soon as he returned to the motel and called Leon at once. He was shocked to learn what had happened at the lab. He only hoped that Craig wouldn't understand what he was looking at and would wait for his return to Goddard in order to question him about it.

Hank was pleased with the amount of information Leon was able to decipher from the Chulosian code, as they were now calling it. Between him and the scientists out at Cartagay, they had deciphered almost the entire message but it was still a puzzle as to why the transmissions had stopped.

"Okay, Leon, you know what to do. Use the satlink code and call Doctor McDaniels and Professor Devane at exactly 3:00 a.m. I'll be patched in through the NASA uplink and we'll have a three-way conversation," Hank said.

He thanked Leon for his painstaking work, said goodnight, and hung up the phone. He set the bedside clock to go off at 2:30 and lay back on the pillows, falling asleep almost immediately.

***

Craig sat in first class, sipping a glass of vodka and looking through the documents he had confiscated from Leon. He thought they were very interesting, especially the notes Leon had scribbled in the margins of several of the sheets. From what Craig could tell, Hank and the scientists at Cartagay had stumbled onto what was probably the most significant scientific discovery in the history of the Earth.

He had made up his mind that he would order the scientists from Cartagay Island back to Goddard using the pretense of a program meeting to discuss new experiments with the Hubble telescope. He knew that Hank would be through with this phase of the COSTAR training and would also be at Goddard. He chuckled to himself. He would have all of his ducks in a row. Pulling a pad from his briefcase that lay across the dining tray, he began to jot down a game plan. He would use this information to his fullest advantage. It could prove to be very valuable to the military and the General's plan, and Craig wondered how he would react. And Craig, always looking for ways to further his influence, pondered how he might use this information to acquire the Director's post as the head of NASA.

The plane was crossing over the Grand Canyon as he placed an airphone call to Libby.

***

Leon Beardsley was not without resources. Unbeknownst to most of his fellow students, Leon was a computer hacker of the highest order, but he didn't use his talent for purchasing airline tickets or altering his grades. That would be too easy. He used his computer genius to further his education in ways the other students couldn't even have imagined.

Leon had secretly tapped the university's computer into the system at Goddard. He now had the ability to monitor every transmission and experiment currently running. Not even Hank knew about it. Leon didn't think it would do any harm; in fact, he even loaded a few experiments of his own on the Goddard database. They were buried deep within the hundreds of programs running and could be accessed with a series of passwords that only Leon knew. He was quite proud of this achievement, especially now since he needed to get into the system to continue his work for Doc Stanton.

The next day, Leon was at the console in the university computer lab. It was 2:05 a.m. and he was just about to make the connection with the Goddard database and the Hubble remote telemetry interface program, the software link to the telescope. As it came up on the screen, Leon realized it was already running and receiving data. Quickly he put his own system into motion and began storing the incoming data: it was another message from Chulos.

15

Crayto Shueneenee was a scientist very much like Kamal Tarn, his closest cremboseedee in the Circle of Comastyr. Crayto was aware of Kamal's concern for Peltoran–3 and its inhabitants, and he was also aware of the importance of Kamal's message. He stood before the Corbal Ring, enabling the Cotera Tunnel to project the remainder of Kamal's message, along with a new message of his own.

At that very moment, Kamal stood before the Council of the Circles, pleading for a change in the Circle of Law. If Kamal was not successful, it wouldn't matter, Crayto thought, that he was sending the remainder of Kamal's message along with the Traylocore and Pulsar Fence design so the Peltorans could protect their planet. The vortex began to energize as the holographic image of Peltoran–3 appeared. Crayto projected the message into the Ring and in a moment it was received by the telescope. Crayto would repeat the same message three times to be sure it was received by the people of Peltoran–3.

***

Leon Beardsley sat motionless, watching the images scroll down the screen, line after line. Suddenly, he jerked and pushed his nose to the glass of the computer monitor. "Holy Shit!" he yelled to the empty university lab. "I'll be damned. These guys have been to our planet before."

Another set of images came through and Leon noticed that these were different from any of the others already sent. "Now what the hell does this mean?"

A set of instructions appeared to be some kind of blueprint for modifying a set of headphones. There was the picture and the instructions for that tower again, he thought. The message lasted about fifteen minutes and then repeated twice more. It abruptly stopped as soon as the last image was recorded. Leon was amazed. It would be an all-nighter trying to decipher the meaning of all of this. He needed to call Hank, and if Hank wanted, he would also call the doctors at Cartagay Island.

Leon printed out the entire message and arranged the computer printout on a large table in the lab. He had deciphered most of the message already and with the help of the computer's database, was developing a kind of alphabet of images and symbols to be translated into the English language. He was fascinated by the fact that the Chulosians would even waste their time to contact Earth at all. They seemed to be hundreds of years ahead of us in their technology. As he continued into the next hour, collating and cross-referencing the images, Leon came across the key to the last message.

The image of the headphones and the pictographic directions were all he needed to make the final jump in his understanding. He smiled to himself, proud of his accomplishment. He looked around the room and noticed his knapsack lying on the floor next to one of the computer consoles. He got up, opened it, and rummaged around in one of the pockets for his cassette recorder and headphones. He walked back over to the table with the printouts and concentrated on the one with the instructions for modifying the headphones. As he examined them more closely, he realized that he didn't have the right tools. He needed to get into the electronics lab.

Leon went over to the computer and shut everything down. Gathering up the printouts, his knapsack and cassette recorder and headphones, he left the lab. He took the stairs down two flights to the first floor, headed out a side door, and walked across the courtyard to the electrical engineering labs. He knew what he needed and hoped that one of the labs would be open.

He entered the building through a service entrance door he knew was never locked. He walked down the corridor, trying every lab door; they were all locked. Leon glanced at his watch: almost six a.m. His first class didn't start until 8:30. Two and a half hours. He walked up and down the halls on the first and second floors but the results were the same. He thought of asking one of the custodians to open it for him, but they might ask too many questions. Besides, they would probably have to enter it into the night log and that could mean more trouble trying to explain why he wanted to be in the computer lab so early. Leon walked back outside and headed for the parking lot. Goddard was only fifteen minutes away.

He stopped and bought a take-out cup of coffee at a fast food drive-through and continued on his way, arriving at the Center at 6:25 a.m. A few technicians and engineers who worked there were also entering through the guard gate. Leon flashed his pass and went on through. He parked his car and headed directly to the electronics lab that Doc Stanton used. Leon was very familiar with this area, having cleaned it a hundred times. He walked through the lobby and said good morning to the night guard still on duty. He climbed the stairs two at a time, up to the second floor. He found Hank's lab but the door was locked. No problem, he chuckled; he had his custodian's master keys. He opened the door and went in.

On a workbench inside Hank's lab, Leon found almost everything he needed except for an input jack for his headphones in order to plug them into the computer. He searched all over the lab but without success. Leon slumped into a chair, thinking. Radio Shack didn't open until ten o'clock. He glanced at his watch: only 6:50. He didn't want to wait three more hours. He wanted to call Hank and let him know what he'd discovered the night before. Doc Stanton would be leaving for the NASA lab by eight that morning. He had to figure out a way to make it work.

"The supply room!" he blurted out to no one. He jumped up and headed for the conference area and the supply room next door, remembering that the input jacks on the recorder unit were exactly what he needed for his little modification. He looked up and down the corridor; no one was around. He went in and locked the door.

He pushed the file cabinet aside. The outlet was still there, just as before. He pulled off the key taped to the back of the cabinet and inserted it into the device. He twisted the device out of the wall smiling to himself. "I was right," Leon whispered. "These babies are exactly what I need."

He disconnected the input jacks from inside the outlet plate and tugged on the wires. "Shit!" he yelled. "The fuckers are jammed." He would have to go into the conference room and detach them from the unit inside the vent. He got up and cracked open the supply room door. The hallway was still empty. He glanced at his watch and knew he had to hurry. He left the supply room and walked into the conference area. It was almost seven thirty.

The conference room was empty as Leon entered, tiptoeing around the chairs to the center of the table. Not bothering to remove his shoes, he jumped up on the table, loosened the clips, and pulled the metal vent grill down. He unplugged the two jacks from the unit inside. He thought about pulling the wires through from the conference room side but feared he might be seen. He decided to go back to the supply room and retrieve them there.

Leon replaced the vent grill in the ceiling but as he climbed down from the table, Libby walked into the supply room. She saw that the recorder had been discovered. She looked closer and saw a knapsack leaning against the cabinet. Whoever was there was coming back. She left the supply room and stepped into an office across the hall wanting to see who found the mini-recorder. She waited less than a minute when Leon came around the corner and entered the supply room. Leon Beardsley! What could he want with that equipment?

She stepped out of the office and quietly went into the supply room. Leon was crouched on the floor pulling the wires through the air conditioning ductwork. Libby, as quiet as a mouse, walked up behind the cabinet. "What the hell is going on here, Leon?"

Leon was so startled that he fell backward onto the floor, the wires he was pulling through the wall entangling his legs like spaghetti.

"Ms. Morales…uh…uh…I can explain," he jabbered "Please don't be angry. I…I, ah…I, ah…just needed these jacks for a long distance phone set-up with my computer. I'm sorry I messed with your tape unit, Ms. Morales. Ms. Morales?".

Leon was paralyzed with shock at having been caught. He'd always been wary of Libby, and was sure she would turn him in to Mr. Jeffreys, the facilities manager at the Center, who would fire him over this.

Libby listened to Leon babble. She couldn't believe he'd found her tape unit. What was even harder to believe was that he was sure it was hers.

"Leon, get up! Now! And shut up!" she said with steely authority.

Leon stood up, untangling his feet from the jumble of wire on the floor. He backed himself against the wall and bowed his head like a little boy caught with his hands in the cookie jar.

"Clean up this mess and put everything back the way it was," Libby ordered. "I'll be in the office across the hall. Come in there as soon as you're done. Now hurry," she said, and walked out of the supply room. She crossed the hallway to the office opposite the supply room. The office would be empty all day because the engineer who normally used it was out of town.

Leon pulled the remaining three feet of wire from the wall, stashed the phone jacks in his pocket, reattached the unit and coverplate in the wall, and pushed the file cabinet back to its original position. He picked up his knapsack, left the supply room, and politely knocked on the office door.

Libby opened the door. She motioned him into the room and to a chair she had placed in front of the desk. "Sit over there. You've a lot of explaining to do, young man, and I'd better like your explanation or you'll find yourself out of a job. I want the truth. Do I make myself clear?" Libby walked behind the desk and sat down.

Leon did as he was told and sat down, awaiting interrogation. He glanced at his watch. It was almost 8:00 in the morning. He was going to miss calling Hank.

***

At the Cartagay station, Brian and Edward received the message from Chulos the same time Leon did. They had been feverishly working on the images and had come up with a translation of their own. They had not been able to understand the part about the Traylocore but they had their own interpretation of what they thought it meant. They needed to speak with Doctor Stanton and his new assistant, neither of whom could be located. It was eight in the evening at Cartagay and the doctors were exhausted. They decided to leave a message for the two of them and retired for the night.

***

"Leon, you're in big trouble for interfering with a federal investigation," Libby started, holding her FBI credentials in his face.

"You're…you're FBI," Leon stammered, sure until this moment that she was a spy.

"Now, tell me everything you know," she ordered.

Leon spent the next hour and a half explaining to Libby what they had discovered and how Doctor Stanton felt it should remain a secret until they knew more about the message and what they should do about it.

"Leon, we have to get in touch with Hank, I mean Doctor Stanton, out at the Cape right away. Do you have a number where he can be reached?"

"I have the number for his hotel and the MMU test lab at the Cape. We could try them both. If he's not at either place, we can leave a message and tell him to call as soon as he gets it," Leon suggested.

"I have a better way to reach him." Libby dialed a number in Washington. After three rings the phone was answered. "I would like to order some flowers, please."

"How could you order flow—" Leon was about to say when Libby put her hand over his mouth to shut him up. He got the hint and sat back down.

"What kind of flowers did you have in mind?" asked the voice on the other end.

"A get well bouquet for a sick friend."

"I have just what you need. Would you like to pick them up or have them delivered?" asked the voice.

"Delivered." Libby gave the address for Goddard Center and the office they were presently in.

"The flowers should arrive within the hour," the voice said, and then the line went dead.

Libby hung up the phone and sat back down. The wall clock said 9:30.

"Leon, one of my associates will be here shortly. I want you to tell him exactly what you told me. Is that okay?" Libby asked.

Leon nodded.

She got up from the desk and looked through the window blinds down to the parking lot. Craig was still in California, thank God.

"Would you like some coffee, Leon?" Libby asked.

He nodded so they both went across the hall to the supply room and made a small pot. They went back to the office and about ten minutes later the phone rang. It was the guard at the gate. Tom Moniot from the FBI was there.

"Send him right up," Libby directed. She hung up and called the lobby guard. "Send Agent Moniot straight up to Ray Carter's office."

Leon, Libby, and Tom Moniot spent the next two hours discussing the message from Chulos and Craig Williams' involvement in the murders, extortion and cover-up surrounding the telescope.

"That hitman's getting closer and we have no idea of his identity or his whereabouts." The concern in Libby's voice was obvious.

"And until we figure out Williams' role in all of this, let's keep quiet about the message from Chulos. We need to talk to Doctor Stanton," Moniot suggested. They nodded in agreement.

"Look, it's getting late, so why don't we meet up tomorrow morning here at the Center," suggested Leon, almost dead on his feet. It had been a long night and he needed some rest and some more time to work on the communicator as he called it.

Tom Moniot just laughed. "I can't believe it. Life on another planet, and they're talking to us. My kids are going to get a real kick out of this."

16

Craig Williams sat at the bar, watching the hotel patrons play around the pool. The temperature was almost 100 degrees, but the desert air was dry. He wasn't used to the heat so he'd ordered just a glass of iced water as he waited nervously. A few minutes went by before a tall, muscular man sat on the bar stool next to Craig.

"Mister Williams, General Reynolds is waiting for you. He's seated over there," the man said, pointing towards a table in the corner of the open air restaurant.

Craig turned around to see the General seated with his back towards the bar. He was a big man, almost six four, with broad shoulders and close-cropped graying hair. Craig disliked the General, feeling subservient in his presence.

He picked up his glass and stepped away from the bar. The General's bodyguard remained behind as Craig walked over to the General's table. "Hello, General Reynolds. Thank you for taking the time to see me on such short notice."

"Sit down," the General ordered. "This meeting better be important, Williams. I postponed a golf game with three senators in order to come down here to see you. What's this all about?"

Lieutenant General Arthur Reynolds was the Commander of a top secret research and development facility in California. Known as the China Lake Naval Weapons Center to the public, to those few in the military that knew of its existence, it was called The Mine. Above ground it was an obscure desert testing range that conducted flight tests on new weapons. Below ground, it was a completely different story. The research lab was located in an abandoned borax mine in the northeast quadrant of the weapons center. Its twelve levels descended almost two thousand feet and were almost six hundred feet in diameter. Purposely surrounded by unexploded ordnance, there was only one way in and one way out. No record of its existence appeared on any map.

General Reynolds had been very successful at fooling the media and the public into believing that Area 51 at the Nellis Air Force range in Nevada was involved in top secret aircraft and UFO research, when all the while it was actually going on at China Lake. The Mine consisted of laboratories, machine shops, hi-tech photo labs, and a remote telemetry receiving station that was tied into Vandenberg, TDRS in New Mexico, and Goddard. It was completely self-sufficient.

The General didn't like Craig very much and was glad he had no idea of The Mine's real purpose. Their business dealings had made the General a very rich man, and that was essential to the General's plans. But to the General, Craig Williams was just an unknowing pawn in a much larger game. He likened Craig to a cross between a weasel and the Cheshire cat from *Alice in Wonderland*.

"General, you're not going to believe this. We've had contact from an alien civilization. The communication came through the HST several days ago. It's real hard evidence this time and it's confirmed," Craig said.

"What!" the General said, genuinely flabbergasted. "When did this happen, and where? How many other people know about this? I want to know everything."

The General took a long pull of beer and tilted his chair back slightly on two legs as Craig related what he knew. He produced copies of the printouts he'd taken from Leon and gave them to the General, who looked at them curiously but without comment. Craig told the General about the implications and possible consequences if the story or any of the information were to get into the hands of the media. He wanted the General's help in putting a clamp of secrecy on the whole thing and transfering the entire Hubble program to military jurisdiction.

General Reynolds gathered up the papers Craig had given him and dropped them into a small leather case by the side of his chair. He picked up his mug and chugged down the remaining beer. "Do you have even the slightest idea what this could mean?" the General asked.

"Do *you*?" Craig asked in return. "General, just think. New technologies, new forms of travel. Communication. The list is endless. We have to get control of this. These aliens may hold the answers to a thousand questions. Do you think they may have some relation to the craft we found in Yaphank? The Guys at Brookhaven are still in the dark on that one."

It had been almost a year since the crash of an alien craft in Yaphank, New York. The military was lucky it happened so close to Brookhaven National Laboratory. Because the lab was a top security installation, they were able to scoop up the entire wreckage and take it to the lab for study. The craft was unmanned, but it yielded a very interesting new plastic that became liquid when subjected to a particular frequency of high-volume sound. The General was well aware of the find because, through sleight-of-hand, he'd managed to take command of the investigation. This was fortunate for the General, because if he hadn't, his own secret agenda would have gone down in flames.

"Shut up, Craig. Now listen. How many people are aware of this?" The General straightened up in his chair and leaned closer to Craig.

"As far as I know, General, only four people: Stanton, and Devane and McDaniels at Cartagay Island. And a janitor at Goddard."

"A janitor!" the General exclaimed under his breath. What kind of outfit did this fool Williams run?

"He's just some dumb college kid working at the lab. Nothing to worry about. Anyway, I'm sure that once you take over command of the Hubble program, we'll have no problems with any of them."

General Reynolds leaned back in his chair again, silent for a full minute as he took this all in.

Craig looked at him, puzzled.

"Ahhhhh. Nothing like a cold beer to cool the soul on a hot day," the General said. "Must be near a hundred by now." He laughed and clapped Craig on the back to change the subject. "Got to get used to the heat, Craig, if you want to come and play in my desert," he laughed.

"I don't know how you people can stand it. I could never get used to this," Craig said, pulling out a handkerchief. He dipped it in his glass of ice water and wiped his face.

The General laughed. "I want you to stick around for a day or two, Craig. If this means what I think it means, I want you to meet with some of my people at the weapons center. I'll contact you at the hotel." With that the General rose and walked off.

Craig watched him leave. As the General walked away, he was escorted by two muscular men in brightly colored shorts, loose shirts, and shoulder holsters. They stepped in behind the general and disappeared from view. Bodyguards, Craig thought, signaling the bartender for a beer.

A waitress came over with his beer and placed it before him. Craig savored the frosty glass for a moment, lifted it in the air, and toasted himself. He hadn't told the General everything. Just enough to whet his appetite and get the ball rolling. He was finally in control, and things were going better than planned. He took a long pull of the cold liquid.

***

Leon Beardsley arrived at the Center at 8:00 the next morning. Libby was already at her desk.

"Good morning, Leon. I hope you got some rest last night. I've a feeling that it's going to be a very busy day," she said.

"I'm fine, Ms. Morales."

"You can call me Libby, Leon. No need for us to be formal around here. How did you make out with your communicator thing there?" She pointed to the small box Leon carried under his arm.

"I think it'll work, but first I need to test it out. When are we going to call Doc Stanton?"

"Right now. Why don't you take a seat and I'll place the call."

Leon sat in a chair next to Libby's desk as she punched in the number for Hank's motel.

He answered on the third ring. "Hello. This is Doctor Stanton."

"Hello, Doctor Stanton. This is Libby Morales at Goddard. Do you have a few minutes? There's someone here who needs to talk with you," she said, and passed the phone to Leon.

"Hello, Doc, it's Leon. There's been a slight change in plans back here."

Hank was concerned as he sat in the motel room in Florida. What was Leon doing with Libby at the Center? Did she know what was going on? Who's side was she on? Questions raced through his mind.

"Doc, you still there?" Leon asked.

"Yeah, I'm still here, Leon. What's going on back there? Can you talk? Why is Libby there? Does she know what's going on?"

Leon sensed the immediacy in Hank's voice. Leon turned toward Libby with a bewildered look. He didn't know what to say.

She took the phone from Leon. "Hank, this is Libby."

"Hi, Libby. Maybe you can tell me what's going on up there?"

"Hank, maybe I should start at the beginning. I found Leon in the supply room, fooling around with a small tape recorder of mine."

"Libby, that thing in there was yours?" There was surprise in Hank's voice.

"Yes, Hank. It was mine. I have to level with you. I'm a field agent for the FBI and I've been working undercover at the Center for almost a year now. We're investigating the possibility of corruption, extortion, fraud, and collusion. We believe it involves Craig Williams and several of the contractors that have worked on the telescope. We also think that several recent homicides can be tied to this investigation."

"Are you serious, Libby?" Hank asked.

"Very serious, Hank, and in light of what Leon has told me about your little discovery, I think you're going to need my help." The phone line was silent. Libby hoped that Hank would understand and recognize the situation they were in.

"Little discovery!" he yelled. "Libby, what has Leon told you?"

"I didn't mean to underestimate what you have stumbled on, Doctor. I apologize for seeming disrespectful. Leon has told me everything, most of which I don't understand. It all sounds like science fiction to me, but I do believe you and your associates have made a remarkable scientific find here," Libby said.

"I'm sorry for snapping at you, Libby. It's been a grueling week for all of us here at the Cape. Have you spoken to McDaniels or Devane out at Cartagay?" he asked.

"I didn't want to call them until I spoke with you first, Hank. I think it important for all of you to meet at the Center and decide the proper course of action. Leon has informed me that Craig Williams may be aware of this discovery and we can't be sure what he's capable of. He's still in California and not due back for another two days. I can arrange for Doctor McDaniels and Professor Devane to be here within twenty-four hours. Can you leave the Cape by tomorrow evening and meet with us here at the Center?" she asked.

"Yes, Libby. I think I can wrap things up here by tomorrow and hop a military flight back to Goddard by the afternoon. You make the arrangements for the doctors at Cartagay to be there. Libby, it's imperative that we keep a lid on all of this until we can decide what's the best way to proceed. Do you agree?" Hank asked.

"Yes, Hank, I agree. Leon will remain with me here, and tonight I think it best if he stay at my house. Just to play it safe,"

Leon, sitting across from the desk was smiling from ear to ear. Libby was the most beautiful woman he had ever seen.

Libby knew what he was thinking and she smiled as she shook her index finger at him in a scolding manner. "Don't even think about it," she mouthed.

Leon smiled ruefully.

"Good idea, Libby. Well, I have to get back to the MMU lab. If you need me, here's the number where I'll be all day," Hank said, and gave Libby the number.

She jotted it down on a notepad on the desk. "Hank, be careful," Libby said, concerned. "There's something else you need to know."

"What's that, Libby?"

"We're convinced that there's a hired killer out there. We think he's working for Craig Williams, but as of now, we can't prove it. We think you may be his next target. It might be wise to provide you with some protection until you return to Goddard."

"Libby, I'm at the Cape. The security here is as tight as it gets anywhere. If anyone wanted to get at me on the base, he'd have to be crazy. Once I leave the motel, I'll be at the base and I'll stay there until I leave tomorrow. How does that sound?" he asked.

"That's fine, Hank. Just stay there until you leave. I'll breathe a lot easier once we have this guy in custody. And Hank, please be careful. This guy is *very* dangerous."

"Okay, Libby. I'll see you tomorrow."

"Bye, Hank," Libby replied, and they both hung up.

***

Craig Williams was back in his hotel room. He needed to place a secured call to Cartagay Island. He went to the closet and took an aluminum briefcase down from the shelf. He placed it on the bed by the phone. He took the phone from the bedside table and disconnected the wire. He then opened the briefcase and plugged the phone wire into an outlet inside the case. The device was a secret encrypting satellite uplink telephone. If anyone tried to tap into the line, all they would hear would be a high-pitched whine. Only the person at the other end could understand what was being said.

Craig thought of General Reynolds as he dialed the number. The phone was a gift from the General in return for services rendered. The line connected and Edward Devane answered.

"Hello. This is Professor Devane. Is this Libby?"

"Hello, Professor. No, this is Craig Williams. How are you and Doctor McDaniels coming with your research?" Craig was curious; why would Devane be expecting a call from Libby?

"Oh, hello, Mister Williams. I was expecting a call from Ms. Morales. She called about an hour ago but we were in the middle of a test and couldn't talk. Working on projects, you know." Devane was caught off guard. He wasn't expecting a call from Craig Williams. Libby *had* called about an hour ago but they were both in the middle of a test and thought it best if she call back in about an hour. Doctor Stanton had briefed them on the possibility of Craig Williams taking the whole discovery and turning it over to the military. If that was the purpose of this call, they would resign in protest.

"Professor, I understand that you and Doctor McDaniels are in the middle of several experiments, but something has come up at Goddard Center and I need you both here by tomorrow. A private jet will be arriving there today to collect you both. You should be in Maryland in about fourteen hours. I hope that this inconvenience will not interrupt your work for more than a day or two, but it is imperative that you both attend a very important meeting at the Center." Craig knew he had them. It would be impossible for them to refuse.

"Mister Williams, I hope you don't mind my asking, but what could be so important that it would make us leave in the middle of our research? I'm sorry, sir, but we must respectfully decline your invitation. You must postpone this meeting until we can make the time to be there," Devane said. He hoped that by stalling it would give them time to contact Doctor Stanton and find out what was going on back in the states.

"Professor Devane, sir, with all due respect, I do mind. This isn't a request, it's an order. As director of this project and your superior in all matters pertaining to it, I am ordering you both to be on that plane. Don't disappoint me or you'll both be rowing home. Do you understand me, sir?" Craig said, raising his voice for emphasis.

"There's no reason to shout, Mister Williams. Our work here is very important to us and to NASA as well. I was just hoping that we might be able to finish a particular experiment we've been working on for the past few weeks. That's all."

"Excuse me, Professor. I didn't mean any disrespect to you or your colleague. Your presence is necessary at Goddard so we may supply you with some new information regarding the COSTAR mission. Doctor Stanton and several of his colleagues will also be there for the briefing," Craig lied.

"Well, that's different, Mister Williams. We would be happy to attend and lend our support. Of course we will be on the plane when it arrives. See you tomorrow evening. Good-bye." He hung up. Devane ran from the office and down the stairs, heading for the telemetry dome.

Craig was satisfied. He had only a few other loose ends to tie up and he would be set. He placed a call to the Marriot Hotel in Daytona Beach, asking the operator for a Mr. Dave Smith in room 907. A voice answered. "Yeah."

"Go for the Cape," Craig said, and hung up.

***

Paul Gaynor, aka Dave Smith, hung up the phone. He checked his watch. He still had plenty of time to make it down to Cocoa Beach, take care of business, and be back in Daytona in time for the night life. He liked the bars and the women. Something about the tanned bodies, he laughed to himself.

Paul went down to his rental car and removed a small case from the trunk and brought it up to the room. Anyone looking at it would have thought he was a trumpet player in the house band. Inside was a modified Spector 9mm sniper machine pistol, one of the most accurate guns in the world. He took it out of the case and checked its components. Satisfied that everything was okay, he loaded an eight-shot magazine into the grip.

He wiped the outside of the gun with a chamois cloth and re-placed it in the case. He checked his watch again. It was almost noon. Riding the elevator down to the lobby, he thought how much he liked Daytona Beach and that when the time was right, he might just buy a house and retire here. He put the pistol case back in the trunk and drove silently out of the hotel garage. He turned the radio on to a local Country station.

Cape Canaveral and the Kennedy Space Center is a sprawling 10,000-acre complex on the east coast of Florida. Only one public access road, NASA Parkway, leads into the complex. A beach road off U.S. Highway 1 runs on the north side of the base complex and is closed to the public during launches. It curves through the Merrit Island National Wildlife Sanctuary and is often crowded with tourists or beachgoers. The beach road has several turn-outs that provide an excellent but distant view of pad 39A, one of the primary launch sites for the space shuttle. South of the beach turn-off is the shuttle vehicle assembly building and the crawlerway used to transport the giant shuttles to the pad. Most of the base is off-limits to the public.

Gaynor parked his rental car on one of the side roads, in the gravel driveway of a small building. A sign on the side of the structure had large black letters that read NOAA. Gaynor knew it was a weather moni-toring station and was only manned during a launch.

This afternoon it was empty. He popped the trunk open and got out of the car. He pulled a pair of white coveralls from a small bag and put them on. The suit had the insignias and patches of a NASA em-ployee, plus an identification badge with his picture on it. The name DAVE SMITH was printed in bold black letters. He took the pistol out of its case, closed the trunk, and got back into the car. Gaynor re-turned to the service road and drove onto the base.

Hank had just finished his turn in the tank. He got on the elevator platform and was lifted out of the pool. The MMU suit he wore weighed over 100 pounds and he had to be assisted by two technicians, one on either side. They unbuckled the heavy space backpack and loaded it onto a cart. Then they opened up Hank's space suit and helped him out of it.

Mark Ramius, also a veteran astronaut, was suited up and awaiting his turn in the pool. Hank walked over to him and wished him good luck. Ramius gave the thumbs-up sign and Hank returned the gesture. Ramius stepped onto the platform and was lowered into the pool. Two divers were in the water waiting for him. The platform descended to thirty feet and stopped at the bottom of the pool. Hank stood for a moment, watching his partner prepare to go through the same exercise he had just completed. Satisfied that everything was okay, Hank went to the locker room to change.

As Hank was changing in the locker room, Gaynor pulled up to the employee entrance to the space center. There were three cars ahead of him on the road leading into the base. The guard checked the credentials of each person as they entered the base. There were, in fact, four different checkpoints after the main entrance. Security was always tight, launch or not. Gaynor checked out the surroundings as he waited in line for the gate. The other cars moved on and he drove up to the guard shack.

"ID, please," the guard said.

"Sure thing," Gaynor replied and handed him his ID.

"Thanks. Have a good one," the guard said, after giving the ID the once-over. Several cars had pulled behind Gaynor's and the next one pulled up to the gate. Gaynor had timed his entrance well; the gate was busy and the guard hurriedly checked everyone through.

Gaynor had a small map of the base in the visor overhead. He pulled it down and double-checked his destination. He put it back and headed for the MMU test lab and pool facility.

***

Hank had finished changing his clothes in the locker room and was deciding whether to go have a snack at the cafeteria or catch Ramius testing in the pool. He opted for the snack. He would be catching a late afternoon military transport flight back to Washington National Airport and didn't know if he would have time to eat. He thought of having dinner with Libby. A warm tingle washed over him at the thought of her voluptuous body. Knowing that she was an undercover FBI agent made her all the more intriguing. He placed his jetbag in the locker and went out to the cafeteria.

Paul Gaynor sat in his rental car with the engine running outside the MMU test pool building. He was in luck, he thought. Hank Stanton had just stepped out of the side door and headed toward the cafeteria building across the parking lot. On the seat beside him was the Spector pistol. He took the gun and checked the sight. He crouched down and pressed the automatic window button. The window slid down silently and Gaynor placed the gun over the edge of the car door.

Hank never noticed the car, or Paul Gaynor. He continued walking across the lot as a guard walking out of the cafeteria stopped to say hello.

"Hi, Doctor Stanton. How goes it in the dunk tank?" he asked. Everyone kidded about the MMU pool.

"Fine, Steve," Hank answered. He knew most of the guards on the base. "How's the food today?"

"Same as always, Doc. Today it's the house special, meteor loaf."

"Thanks for the warning. I think I'll just have a sandwich and a cup of coffee and play it safe," he said.

"Good idea, Doc. I can see your education has really paid off."

They both laughed.

"Damn!" the guard muttered. "No matter how many times I tell these people, they still can't get it straight. Look at that car parked over there." He pointed at Paul Gaynor's rental car. "Parked in a reserved space. Excuse me, Doc, I have to find out whose car that is and get them to move it before I catch hell from some bigshot." He waved good-bye and walked toward the car.

Gaynor was crouched low and didn't hear the conversation between the guard and Hank. When he lifted his head up to see again, the guard was almost on top of him. The guard saw the gun leaning on the window ledge of the car door. He froze for a moment too long and then instinctively reached for his service revolver. It was too late; Gaynor squeezed off two rounds that ripped into his chest and sent him hurtling backward.

Hank turned around just as the guard was hit. The cafeteria dumpster was next to the back doorway Hank was going to use. As Gaynor took aim, Hank leaped for cover. Four shots ricocheted noisily off the dumpster's steel side, alerting one of the cooks inside the cafeteria. He reacted to the sight of Gaynor's gun by pulling the handle for the kitchen fire alarm. A deafening siren went off in the cafeteria, joined by several others close by.

Gaynor dropped the gun in the passenger footwell and slid back over to the driver's seat. He slammed the car into reverse and was gone before Hank could get the plate number. Gaynor reached the main gate in less than a minute, driving with one hand on the wheel and the other on the pistol, just in case. The main gate guard, thinking the sirens were for a kitchen fire, waved him through.

Gaynor raced down the service road to the small building he stopped at before. A gray government pick-up truck was in the driveway. He jumped out, removed his coveralls, tossed them into the bushes, and quietly worked his way up to the window.

A technician inside was intently working on a piece of equipment and hadn't noticed Gaynor drive up. He took the silenced pistol out of his coat and stepped inside. The young man had his back to the door and died instantly with a single shot to the head. Gaynor rifled his pockets and found the key to the truck. He left the weather station, moved the rental car around the back of the building, climbed into the pick-up, and calmly drove back to his hotel in Daytona.

This Stanton guy must have a lucky charm, he thought, tuning the truck radio into the local Country station. I'll catch up with him in Maryland. Much more convenient that way. After he'd got rid of Stanton, he would retire to a nice place on the beach. He'd had it with this business. Maybe his luck was running out. Maybe it was time to hang up the guns and seek some other line of work. Like a beach bum, he laughed, thinking about lean, tanned bodies in white bikinis.

He reached the hotel an hour and a half later and left the gray truck in the underground parking area. He checked out, took a shuttle bus to the airport in Orlando, and caught the next flight to Washington, DC.

***

Craig was working on his notes when the phone rang. It was one of the General's aides; a car was enroute to the hotel and would arrive within the hour. Although Craig was aware of some of the research at China Lake, he had no knowledge of what was going on at The Mine. The car arrived, and two hours later they drove up to the inconspicuous entrance of the military's most closely guarded secret facility. The Mine's primary focus was supposed to be weapons' research, but actually the people there were engaged in the full-time study of extraterrestrial life.

The Mine was very cleverly concealed, both from satellite surveillance and any possible ground intruders. General Reynolds had even hired a fictitious guard force to patrol Area 51 at Nellis. His masquerade worked perfectly. The media and the UFO nuts, as he called them, kept a constant vigil out there. The General even went so far as covering an F-117 Stealth Fighter in blinking Christmas lights and flying it into Area 51 just to keep the flying saucer watchers happy. It worked every time.

The car drove down a long ramp almost fifty feet below the ground. It came to a stop near a bank of elevators. The General was waiting. He greeted Craig and motioned for him to step into one of the elevators. Craig noticed the panel inside the elevator had only two buttons, up and down. They descended quickly to the first level, thirteen hundred feet below the China Lake desert. The doors opened and they stepped out. Waiting just outside was an electric car with a smartly dressed lieutenant in attendance.

"We'll take it from here, Lieutenant Stevens, thank you," the General said, saluting. The young officer returned the salute and stepped into the elevator.

"Get in, Craig. I think it's time I showed you my little kingdom under the sand," said the General, as they climbed into the car and headed down a long corridor.

They drove on until the corridor opened onto a wide, cavernous room. Craig was amazed at the enormity of the place. He saw what looked like laboratories, machine shops, living quarters, and even a recreation area.

What really caught his attention was the strange craft suspended from a scaffold in the center of the work area. Craig had never seen anything like it. He wondered what it was. The General, seeing the look of astonishment on Craig's face, laughed. "We call it Diamond Mace, Craig. It's a microwave lightcraft."

17

The attack at the Cape had left a guard and a technician dead. Hank was more angry than shaken by the ordeal. The FBI had swarmed over the base. They told Hank the killer had escaped and was probably already out of the state. Two agents were assigned to stay with him as bodyguards until he returned to Goddard.

"Yes, I understand Libby…We're taking every precaution…There are two agents here now…I'll be leaving within the hour…Okay…Yes. I will…See you in a few hours…Bye," Hank said, and hung up the phone.

The news was being played down by the press people at NASA. They described the murders as the work of a disgruntled and crazed former employee. No mention was made of the other homicides. Hank Stanton just happened to be in the wrong place at the wrong time, they said. The media bought the story. Libby and the other agents in Maryland had a good description of the killer from the main gate guard at NASA, but they still didn't know his identity. Hank had only caught a fleeting glimpse of the killer crouched in the car. Libby knew that Hank was still a target and the next attempt would probably go down in Maryland. What worried her was the fact that Hank wasn't the kind of guy who would sit still in protective custody. Besides, if Hank dropped from sight they might never catch this guy. She hated these kinds of manhunts; anything could happen, and it usually did.

***

Hank grabbed his flight bag from the tarmac, climbed the ladder to board the military C-130 transport, and took a seat near the window. The flight from Cape Canaveral air station to Maryland would take about two and a half hours.

As the engines revved up to take off speed, he glanced out at pad 39A. The shuttle *Columbia* was on station, awaiting its next flight. A

feeling of excitement ran through him as he thought about the up-
coming COSTAR mission. Until now, the telescope and the Chulosian
discovery had filled his thoughts, but in the last few hours it seemed as
though the whole world had gone crazy. Hank couldn't believe that
someone was trying to kill him. Could Libby be right? Is Craig Williams really involved? Even though Hank loathed the man professionally,
he couldn't believe Craig would resort to murder.

He tried to change his frame of thought and concentrate on the
telescope's discovery instead. He had a myriad of things to do back at
the Center. He needed to meet with Leon and Libby and to make
contact with McDaniels and Devane. It was imperative that they come
to Goddard Center at once. There was so much to do. Hank would
have to break the news of this discovery to NASA director, Dan Silver,
who would in turn notify the NSC and the President. He wondered
what their reaction would be. The news of the Chulosians would change
the world forever.

***

In all the confusion out at the Cape, Libby hadn't returned the call
to the scientists at Cartagay Island. In Craig Williams' office, she looked
for evidence that might tie him, and possibly, others to the case. She
picked up the phone and dialed the receiving station in the Pacific.
The phone rang six times before it was finally answered by one of the
technicians. Libby found out that the two scientists, on orders from
Craig Williams, had left over four hours ago, on their way to Maryland in a military jet sent by General Arthur Reynolds.

The hairs on her neck prickled. Her sixth sense for danger told her
that something was going down. Why would Craig order the scientists
to Goddard? What excuse could he have used? She realized she was
still holding the phone in her hand and set it back in the cradle. She
thought for a moment, picked the phone up again and dialed Tom
Moniot, this time on the direct line.

"Hello, Tom. Libby. Williams has ordered the scientists from
Cartagay Island back to Maryland. They're on a plane right now and
should be here sometime tomorrow afternoon. I don't like it. Craig

Williams is in California and can't be reached. I'll bet by tomorrow he'll be back at the office acting as though it's business as usual. We have to nab this bastard before our elusive Mr. Smith decides to pay us another visit."

"We'll start closing the net. When is Doctor Stanton due back at the Center?" Tom asked.

"He should be here within the hour. Agents Reed and Cochran are with him and will provide escort back to Goddard. I'll call you as soon as he arrives."

"Thanks, Libby. Don't worry. I have a feeling this case is going to be wrapped up soon. This creep Smith, or whatever his name is, seems to be getting sloppy. He's going to slip up and we're going to grab him. We're following leads from six different states. It's only a matter of time until he walks into our trap."

"I hope so, Tom. It would be a disaster if he got close to Hank," Libby said.

There was more than FBI concern in her voice, Tom noticed but said nothing. He smiled at the phone, thinking of Libby and Doctor Stanton. He wondered what their kids would look like.

***

Six hours after visiting The Mine, Craig Williams was back in his hotel room, still reeling from what he had seen. The Diamond Mace Project had developed a microwave lightcraft capable of speeds in excess of 33,000 mph. Craig thought that the technology to produce such a craft was at least 50 to 100 years away. He pressed the General for more specific information on the craft, but his reaction was only to be more vague. The General had made it quite clear to Craig that he would assume management of the Hubble project and have it moved to The Mine.

As Craig sat in his hotel room pondering how he might profit from this association, General Arthur Reynolds made a very long distance call to a spacecraft in stationary orbit on the dark side of the Moon. It was the primary vessel of the Eltorum Shayloree, a race of reptilian shape-shifters who had established a permanent base on the

Moon nearly three years earlier. As the General relayed what he knew about the recent discovery by the Hubble, it was evident that the contact with the Chulosians had caught everyone off guard. A change in plans was necessary.

Aboard the Eltorum command ship, Sataran, their commander instructed General Reynolds on how to proceed. What he didn't tell him was that the Eltorum had only one enemy in the universe—the Chulosians and their power of the GEE.

The Eltorum had been coming to Earth for generations from their home planet, Eltor, 70 light years from Earth. Their purpose was simple: enslavement of Earth's people and the ravaging of the planet's natural resources. To them, the Earth was only a way station, a stopping off point in their conquest of the known inhabited planets. They had been thwarted by the peaceful Chulosians before and were powerless against them. It had been nearly four thousand Earth years since they had last encountered them on planet Earth.

General Reynolds knew he would have to enlist the support of some of his colleagues on the Joint Chiefs at the Pentagon. Three of them were already associates of the Eltorum. With the promise of wealth and power, they were easy prey for the aliens. General Reynolds also knew he would have to gain the approval of the President in order to carry out his next move. He wasted no time putting his plan in motion.

***

Craig boarded his flight for Washington, DC, at 9:00 Pacific time. It would take almost six hours for the flight back and he didn't want to waste a moment. The fact that Stanton was still alive had almost brought his plans to a screeching halt. He wondered if the fabled hit man was losing his touch and toyed with the idea of calling General Reynolds and asking for a replacement.

As Craig boarded the plane, he didn't notice the man and woman who had been following him since he checked in at the ticket counter and were now two rows behind him in the first class section. He sat back, read a few magazines, and watched the in-flight movie. He had to laugh; the movie was *Independence Day*.

The aircraft landed ten minutes ahead of schedule. As Craig stood at the baggage carousel, the man and woman disappeared into the crowd and were replaced by two young men in hiking clothes who looked as though they had just returned from a camping trip to Colorado. Craig picked up his car and drove out of the airport. The two young men followed three car lengths behind.

Craig pulled into the driveway of his suburban townhouse and activated the electric garage door opener. The device engaged with a whine and swung the door upwards. He pulled his car inside as the door came down behind him.

Inside an unmarked white van parked across the street, two FBI agents checked their electronic listening devices. The two hikers in the car that had followed Craig from the airport drove by the van slowly. The radio crackled as one of the hikers checked in and gave his report. The two agents in the van acknowledged the hand-off and said goodnight to their fellow agents in the car. The hikers drove down the street and were gone. A green light on one of the van's equipment panels flashed on.

"Here we go, Larry. He's on the phone," the agent sitting at the console said. The other agent picked up a pair of headphones and they both listened in on Craig Williams' conversation as two tape machines made a permanent copy.

***

The private jet landed at Washington National Airport at nine o'clock in the evening. Because Cartagay is an American territory, it was not necessary for the two scientists to go through Customs. In any case, the FBI was there in force. Libby was in the lead car that pulled out onto the taxiway and met the jet. As it came to a stop and the door opened, she got out of the car to greet the scientists.

They had been in the air for almost fifteen hours since leaving Cartagay Island and both looked a little worse for wear. Brian McDaniels stepped out of the plane first, followed by Edward Devane. Each carried an overnight bag and a briefcase.

Libby walked over to the two distinguished scientists and introduced herself. Although they had talked on the phone many times, they had never met. "Hello, Doctor McDaniels. I'm Libby Morales." She recognized them from photographs.

"Hello, Libby. We finally get to meet the person behind that lovely voice," McDaniels said.

Doctor Brian McDaniels was a kind and scholarly gentleman of almost sixty years. He was short in stature, standing only about five six. He reminded Libby of the movie actor Sebastion Cabot. He had the disposition of a kind grandfather. Professor Edward Devane on the other hand was much younger. Libby knew he was in his late forties. He was a lanky man with thick glasses and a hearing aid in each ear, the result of a lab accident many years ago.

"Is this Libby Morales?" Edward asked stepping in behind his colleague, peering through the Coke bottle lenses. "My, my, Libby. You have exceeded my wildest expectations," he said, beaming at her.

Both scientists were poking each other like school kids. Then they noticed three large black cars parked around the plane and several men in suits with guns drawn and at the ready. They looked quizzically at Libby.

She saw the concern on their faces. "Just a precaution, gentlemen," she reassured them. "Now if you will please get in the car I'll explain on the way to the Center."

Their puzzled frowns grew when they noticed the long chain around Libby's neck and her FBI credentials. Libby got in the front passenger seat as agents held the rear doors for the scientists. They left the airport in a small motorcade and headed for Goddard Center, where Hank and Leon were already waiting.

***

"I'm impressed, Leon. If we interface this with the Hubble comlink and bounce the signal off of the Starmapper Deep Space Probe, we should be able to use the same type of gravity wave interpolation to send a message back to Chulos," Hank said. They were in the Space Science Lab examining the communication device that Leon had fabricated.

He checked several sheets of telemetry data they had prepared for the other scientists to examine.

"Yeah, it all sounds great, Doc, but Starmapper is the key. It's still on course, about three days away from Mars. How are we going to get permission for a course correction that will catapult the satellite around the planet and send it halfway across the galaxy to Chulos?"

The young student had come up with a plan that would allow real time communication with a planet over 162 trillion miles away. At first Hank thought it would be impossible to accomplish, yet as he pored over Leon's calculations, he realized that maybe they *could* do it.

Leon's plan was to send a coded radio signal to NASA's Starmapper and cause it to alter course. Instead of positioning itself on a course that would send it to the planet Mars, the signal would direct it to Jupiter. The gravitational pull of the giant planet would act like a slingshot to hurtle the spacecraft on a course towards Chulos. According to the message from the Chulosians, they could skim the satellite across the tops of the gravitational waves that constantly roll through the galaxy. These would propel the spacecraft at speeds they could only imagine. Hank believed it would work, but that would be the easy part. The hard part would be getting permission to commandeer a multi-million dollar piece of hardware. Hank figured that the President would have to be the one to give the okay and explain to Congress and the public that it had exploded in space. Hank thought the media would buy the story but that it would result in a lot of 'NASA bashing,' a very small price to pay in light of this discovery.

"Doc, you know something's still bothering me about all of this," Leon said.

"Yes, Leon. What's that?"

"Even if we can get the Starmapper to act as a linear amplifier and we do actually contact the Chulosians, what are we going to say?"

"I don't know. I don't think they would understand a simple, 'Hi, how are you?' We might be better off projecting digital pictures, or something like that. I really don't know, Leon. I think we'll have to play that one by ear."

Leon's question bothered him because the answer eluded him. He looked at the printouts of the images sent by the Chulosians. The image of a large exploding star stood out vividly in color from the laser printer. Planet Earth was directly in the path of what seemed to be an immense pulse of radiation. Another image was of some kind of tower assembly that was shown at the North and South Poles. Was this something that could protect the planet from whatever that pulse was?

They needed more information, and since they'd had no further contact with Chulos, it was imperative that they communicate with them somehow. Right now Starmapper was the only answer.

***

The scientists arrived at Goddard Center at 11:30. The four agents who had accompanied them in the small motorcade left. Libby and Tom Moniot continued with the scientists, going immediately to the Space Science Lab. After the greetings and introductions were through, Hank and the scientists began the business of comparing notes and drawing up a game plan.

"Libby, it looks like we're going to be working here most of the night. Do you think it would be possible to get some coffee and sandwiches?" Hank asked on behalf of himself and the other scientists.

"Sure, Hank. I'll go over to Denny's and get some take-out," Libby said.

"Yeah, Doc, I'm starved too. I think I'll go with Ms. Morales and give her a hand while you guys go over your notes. Okay?"

"Sure, Leon go ahead. We'll be going over these documents for the next hour anyway."

"Okay, Doc, we'll be back soon."

Libby waved good-bye to the three men and smiled affectionately at Hank. He smiled back and gave her a wink and a thumbs-up sign. Libby beamed, still a little puzzled by the chemistry building between them. Tom must have read her mind because, as they walked outside to the car, he leaned over and said to Libby, "He's a good catch, you know."

"I know, Tom," she answered, blushing. The more she was around Hank the more she wanted him. She hoped they would soon get the chance to be alone.

Libby, Tom, and Leon got in the car and headed out, stopping at the guardhouse to notify the guard where they were going. As they left the gate, talking and laughing, none of them noticed the guard pick up the phone.

***

Craig dialed the number for the hotel. Gaynor picked it up on the first ring. "Change in plans. We have a snake in our midst and only a weasel can catch it. The name is Libby Morales. She *used* to be my secretary. I just found out she's a federal agent. She has to be eliminated, and *now*. When I hang up, connect your fax machine to the phone and I'll send you her picture. You'll need to hurry. My source at Goddard said they just left for the Denny's on Broadview. Don't slip up this time. I want it clean and final."

"No problem," Gaynor said, hanging up the phone.

He got up from the motel bed and retrieved a small portable fax machine from his suitcase. Placing it on the bedside table, he unplugged the wire from the back of the motel phone, inserted the connector into the fax machine, and in less than a minute had a picture of Libby Morales. As he studied it, he savored the kill and the sound of bullets entering human flesh.

He leaned over the bed and grabbed his case with the Spector 9mm pistol. He opened it and checked the four new clips he had put in the pocket of the case. Each magazine held 16 bullets. Also in the case was a red helium/neon laser scope. He took it out of its protective sheath and mounted it on the weapon. More than enough for the job, he thought.

He took one more look at Libby's picture, folded it twice, and slipped it into his jacket pocket. He picked up the gun case and left the motel. This time he would be sure. No mistakes and no margin for error. Spray the area with bullets and everything goes down. A certain kill.

He knew exactly where the restaurant was. Less than a five-minute drive. He left the parking lot, tuning the radio to Country music and thinking of the beach in Florida and all those lean, tanned bodies. He wanted to get back there as soon as this job was through. As he drove, he day-dreamed of a beachfront house and a pair of binoculars. Girl-watching was the closest thing he had to a hobby.

***

Libby, Leon, and Tom Moniot entered the restauraunt and sat in a corner booth. A waitress took their order and returned a minute later with three cups of coffee. Libby asked the waitress for three roast beef sandwiches and three containers of coffee to go. The waitress wrote a separate ticket for the take-out order and went back into the kitchen. Tom and Libby engaged in small talk while Leon read the late edition of the newspaper. None of them noticed a car pull into the space behind theirs.

Craig had given Gaynor a description of the car they were driving on the fax. It was late so only a few cars were in the lot. Gaynor saw their vehicle and slowly positioned his car in the space behind it. He could see the three of them through the window of the restaurant. He waited, the machine pistol nestled in his lap. Finally they got up to leave.

"I'll get the check, Libby. Why don't you and Leon get the car. Here, you take the sandwiches and, Leon, you take the coffee," Tom said.

Libby and Leon walked outside and stood at the entrance for a moment. Libby's hair prickled on her neck. She looked at Leon and then back inside the restaurant at Tom, still standing at the counter. She turned and looked around the parking lot and counted the cars. There were seven cars when they had pulled in, and now there were eight. The additional car was parked directly behind theirs. Libby didn't recall anyone entering the restaurant after them.

Gaynor crouched motionless behind the car. He saw his target and a young black man at the entrance to the restaurant. Inside, the other man was at the counter. Gaynor needed them to be closer; he wanted to get the man inside. He waited. What was she doing? he wondered.

Libby waited for Tom. She couldn't see any movement in the parking lot. Maybe she was wrong about the number of cars; she wasn't paying that much attention when they had arrived.

Leon stepped off of the curb and started for the car. Libby, who was walking about three feet behind him, stopped and turned towards the restaurant. The manager finally came out and Tom was paying the bill. She continued back to the car. Leon was almost fifteen feet in front of her.

Gaynor watched as the young black kid got closer. He walked up to the passenger side and was momentarily out of sight. No matter, Gaynor thought. First the girl, then the older guy as he comes out, and then the kid. He'll be scared shitless anyway. Like sitting ducks. Gaynor chuckled silently.

As Leon reached for the passenger door, he realized it was still locked so he had to wait for Libby. She walked to the driver's side. Her hand was in her purse, her finger on the trigger of her .357 magnum service revolver. It wasn't a very large weapon but it packed a punch, she thought, thumbing the safety off.

Gaynor watched Moniot leave the diner and head for the car. It was now or never, he thought, crawling around to the side of his car for a clear shot at Libby. At the same moment, out of Gaynor's line of sight, Leon walked behind the car. He saw the glint of Gaynor's weapon in the glow of the parking lot lights. "Hey, whatchu doin' there?" he called out.

A split second later Libby saw Gaynor, too, crouched low on the ground near the front of the other car. She dropped to the ground as Gaynor let off a burst of bullets that went high. Tom drew his gun just as the startled Gaynor turned and fired another hail of bullets. The front windows of the restaurant exploded as bullets smashed through the glass. The few people inside screamed as glass flew everywhere.

Two of the bullets hit Tom Moniot in the arm and leg. He went down shooting his own revolver. One of the bullets shattered the window of Gaynor's car. It was just the distraction Libby needed. Her gun was out and she was looking under the car, hoping for a clear shot. Instead of Gaynor, she saw Leon sneaking around the back of the killer's car. As Leon's feet disappeared and the car sank down a bit, Libby realized he'd climbed onto the trunk. What was he doing?

Libby now saw the assassin crouched against the car's tire. She didn't have a clear shot and if she missed, she would reveal her position. She saw Tom Moniot on the ground near the entrance. In the distance Libby heard the screams of restaurant patrons.

Gaynor knew the girl was on the other side of her car. He had to do this quickly before he got boxed in. He began to turn and slowly rise, looking for a clear shot of the girl and the—suddenly he realized he didn't see the black kid. He jumped up but it was too late. Leon, on top of Gaynor's car, held two of the large cups of steaming coffee. As soon as he saw the man begin to stand, Leon threw the coffee right at Gaynor's face. By the time Gaynor realized what was happening, the coffee was already a steaming arc in the air. He pulled the trigger just as the scalding coffee hit him in the face.

There was a scream. Libby rolled out from behind the car and saw Leon fall onto the ground. She jumped up and squeezed off five shots. Every one hit Gaynor square in the chest. He slumped like a rag doll and went down. A flash of the warm sunny beaches of Florida was the last thought in his mind before he lay dead on the cold parking lot pavement. Libby ran around to the back of the car. She saw the hitman on the ground, blood still pumping from the gaping wounds in his chest. Libby kicked the gun from his lifeless hand.

She then raced around to the back of the car. Leon was hit in the arm; the bullet had creased his shoulder. "Leon, hold down hard with your other hand," she told him.

"What the fuck's goin' on, Libby?" Leon asked.

They were both standing over the body of Paul Gaynor. "Nothing, Leon, It's over. Wait here, I have to go help Tom," she said, racing across the parking lot.

Tom looked worse than he was. One of the bullets had passed through the muscle in his leg, but he wasn't bleeding too badly. The arm wound was superficial. Libby applied pressure to his leg as Leon came over and sat on the ground next to them. Some of the people from the restaurant came out to help as the police arrived.

"You got the bastard, Libby," Tom said through teeth clenching in pain.

"Yeah. I got him alright. That's one *bendayho* we won't have to worry about anymore."

"Ben-what?" Leon asked, joining them by the restaurant door.

"It's a word we have in Puerto Rican for asshole."

"Yeah. Thank God for Puerto Ricans," Leon said.

"Yeah. Thank God," Libby repeated, stroking the back of her neck and looking back at the spot where the dead hitman lay.

As Tom and Leon were loaded into an ambulance, Libby went back to the parking lot and stood over Gaynor's lifeless body.

"You son-of-a-bitch, *bendayho*. Now we go after your boss."

18

The city of Alpore-Tem on the planet Chulos was home to the member families of the Circle of Comastyr. It was a beautiful city of coral-like structures and luminescent brilliance.

The Chulosians lived in floating globes anchored to the bottom of the sea with plant-like roots. Their technology was based on biological mechanics, as opposed to Shoone Peltoran–3's dependence on inorganic machines. All Chulosian machinery was composed of living organisms that were in complete harmony with the natural order of their planet and the entire universe around them. By its very nature, Chulosian bio-technology produced almost no waste. Every by-product of their science was consumed and produced more energy. They had harnessed the power of their star, not by collecting its rays and converting them into some kind of electricity, but by absorption and infusion. Every Chulosian had the ability to capture and unleash enormous power.

Kamal Tarn had been summoned by thought-merge to the Council City of Gee-Corem, the seat of law of the planet Chulos, the city of the Council of the Gee. Kamal had been asked to present his argument for saving Shoone Peltoran–3. He knew that it would be two hundred Peltoran–3 years before they could be allowed contact but the radiation pulse would destroy Shoone Peltoran–3 within one more orbit around its sun. The planet's inhabitants would not survive.

As Kamal entered the circle gate of the city, he saw that many of his fellow scientists had already gathered at the gate awaiting his arrival. They all stood before him, mouths wide open and tongues extended, their bodies changing colors like a kaleidoscope. As Kamal approached each individual, he used his webbed hand to stroke the tongue of each one.

As he stroked their tongues in a gesture of friendship they each bowed in recognition of his achievements. He entered the gate as the procession of other Chulosians gathered in behind him like a marching band about to enter a football field. They filed into the hall of the Council and everyone joined in a circle around their comrade. Council members were seated on the other side of the structure on a semi-circular platform suspended about five feet above the group.

Kamal wore the robe of the Chotor of Comastyr, a sheer cloth that glowed blue, red and yellow, depending on the way light reflected from the fabric. It swayed in the watery expanse that was the atmosphere of Chulos. It appeared to be alive as it swirled in every direction, like some kind of moray eel. The crowd of well-wishers parted to form a semi-circle as Kamal stood before the Council.

He bowed low and opened his mouth wide, the Chulosian gesture for greetings. The Council members rose as one and returned the gesture. The platform lowered and Kamal Tarn approached the circular bench. He reached out and stroked the tongue of each member of the Council. They smiled in a gesture of friendship.

The greeting ceremony over, the Council bench returned to its hovering position. Kamal moved to the center of the Council Chamber. The being standing in the center of the Council ring began to speak. To humans it might sound like the chirping of songbirds. It was actually more like a musical tone, as though the Chulosians were playing flutes.

Kamal stood at the center of the Council awaiting his turn to speak. Normally, the Chulosians spoke by thought-merging, sending mental pictures to each other to communicate what they wanted to say. In the Council Chamber they traditionally spoke out loud in the ancient musical language of their ancestors.

"Your request reminds me of the old times, Kamal, when we were explorers of the Outer Rock Worlds. We were shapers of the universe, as is our mission, handed down by the first Council.

"It is the Law of the GEE that we bring peace to the Outer Rock Worlds. Our gifts have often gone unheeded by many of those that have been given them. You have given a circle in friendship to these rock worlders and they have not responded. It is because they still have the anger of their ancestors, as we have seen on other rock worlds so many times before.

"Kamal, it is dangerous for you and our people to send the images through the Cotera to them. Yes, it is true that we have been to the rock world Shoone Peltoran–3 many times, as have many others that inhabit the outer worlds, including the Eltorum Shayloree. And like the old times, they have again begun to influence the course of Shoone Peltoran–3's future just as they did on Melkos. They have already begun the association of many of Shoone Peltoran–3's inhabitants. Soon it will be too late to reach any of them.

"We have studied their species closely, Kamal. You know first hand the results of our research. They are an aggressive race bent on destruction. Their primitive beliefs will cause them to use our gifts to destroy. We must wait for them to find the power of the GEE. Without it they will never know peace, and so we must pass these rock worlders over until they reach the time of fulfillment. The Council has thought-merged on the question and before we bond the circle, we will allow you to speak on behalf of the inhabitants of Shoone Peltoran–3." The words of the Council Podor, Barseldwyngee rang true for Kamal.

Kamal knew that although many of the beings on Peltoran–3 had unknowingly discovered the power of the GEE, it was still the new time for the inhabitants of the planet. Many generations ago, the people of Peltoran–3 had been marked by the Chulosians with a tagged dormant gene and now the power of the GEE was beginning to awaken in them. He had to convince the Council that they would all perish in the massive radiation storm approaching their planet. He also knew from monitoring their civilization that they were on the threshold of a new age of enlightenment. They must be saved and brought into the circle of the Outer Rock Worlds as friends in the universe. They must be taught how to use the power of the GEE to save their planet from destruction.

"I stand before my family and the Council. In circle thought-merging I have sought an answer that our people will trust. It is true that these rock worlders from Shoone Peltoran–3 are a violent race. But we have planted the power of the GEE in many generations. It is in their blood. This now is a new time, and we are in error. I have seen Shoone Peltoran–3 pass through these past twelve relons and they are coming into the knowledge of the GEE—in small groups, yes—but I have seen the result of this new age of reasoning. It is the next stage of their Awakening that we must save.

"The Law of the GEE and the circle of all of the families demand that we send the Pulsar Fence in the Cotera. We must act soon or it will be too late. I appeal to the Circle. If the Eltorum are permitted to continue, they will enslave this race just as they have done on the other rock worlds and Shoone Peltoran–3 will be lost to us as a friend forever. The time for us to act is now!" Kamal finished and bowed before the Council.

Keltor Cremboseedee of the Circle of Dilothan was seated on the Council of the Gee. He opened his mouth and bowed before the other members of the Council. Keltor was a respected outer world explorer. Although it was his circle that had discovered most of the outer worlds with which the Chulosians now related, Kamal Tarn's Circle of Comastyr had discovered Shoone Peltoran–3.

"I speak for my Chotor and the families of all the houses of Chulos. We cannot be induced to offer merging with these savage Shoone Peltoran–3 people who have already begun to be turned by the Eltorum. If even one of the Shayloree knew of our presence on Shoone Peltoran–3, it could bring great conflict to Chulos. The great battle with the darkness of Eltor, which has been spoken about for many relons by the elders of Chulos, would come to pass. It is not the time, my brothers. We cannot allow the peace of the GEE to be compromised by the dark thought feelings of one rock world. We must think of our pathways into tomorrow. Leave Shoone Peltoran–3 to the Corbal Ring of Infinity. If it is within the power of the GEE to merge with this planet, than it will be spared destruction by either this pulse or the Eltorum. We must not interfere. This, my family, is the merging of our circle and it will not be broken." Keltor ended his speech with a gracious bow and with his mouth opened wide.

Kamal stood off to one side, suspended in the calm ocean of Chulos. Each member of the circles of Chulos, representatives of every Chotor, came before the Council. Kamal was defeated, but he hadn't lost. He knew that if it came to this, he would defy the Circle of the Gee and contact Shoone Peltoran–3 again. He knew the punishment well for defying the Council of Circles: banishment to the rock world Pelnor in the Dralora galaxy. There he would pass into the merging of light and darkness on a world on the other side of a black hole.

The Council made its decree and all present stood as if in suspended animation as the thought picture of the Council touched everyone on the planet. In an instant the entire planet knew of the outcome of the meeting of the Council of Circles and the Circle of the Gee. Kamal Tarn was forbidden any more contact with the rock world Shoone Peltoran–3.

***

Crayto Shueneenee was saddened by the Council decree. He stood at the entrance to the globe of Comastyr, the home of Kamal's circle on Chulos. Kamal entered and they exchanged greetings. In the center of the suspended globe was Kamal Tarn's lab and the Corbal Ring. They were silent as Kamal contemplated his next transmission to Shoone Peltoran–3. Crayto was worried and it showed in the black splotches that kept appearing on his neck and torso. Kamal saw this and extended his hand to scratch the tongue of his associate. The black spots disappeared and were replaced by the normal bluish gray skin tone of the Chulosians.

Kamal took a clear crystal ball and tossed it into the Corbal Ring. Instead of falling or floating away, it remained suspended in the liquid atmosphere. It began to emit a yellow light and the two Chulosians walked to the edge of the ring. They grasped the railing surrounding the Corbal Ring and began to hum. As they did, the crystal globe began to spin faster and faster, until it emitted a yellow light. When the light had dissipated from the crystal, Kamal reached into the ring and took it in his webbed fingers.

"This message goes to a being on the rock world, Shoone Peltoran–3. He will find a way to answer. They *do* have the power of the GEE, Crayto, I can feel it in the merging. I have seen it in the waves of thought they send out to the galaxy."

19

Hank, McDaniels, and Devane were working in the lab when two FBI agents came into the room to tell them about the shoot-out. Everyone was relieved to know that Libby got the hitman and that Tom and Leon would be okay. Hank kept asking about Libby, if she was hurt, if she was coming back to the lab. McDaniels, after being assured that everyone was okay, asked about his sandwich and coffee. Devane was just glad to be in the lab working on the Chulosian message and was oblivious to everything else going on around him.

Once Hank knew that Libby was unharmed, he went back to work on the computer printouts and Leon's design for the communicator. They also made several sample telemetry routes for the Starmapper probe and the data codes required to alter its course. It would not be an easy task, Hank thought, but it could be done. According to the Chulosian messages, time was running out. The scientists wanted everything to be perfect before presenting their findings and recommendtions to the NSC.

They continued working in the lab and checking the current telemetry of the telescope. It had been several days since the last message was received and it concerned them that it had been cut off in midtransmission. Hank checked the wall clock in the lab: almost 2:00 a.m. They all stopped what they were doing in anticipation of another message. Hank sat down at the transmission receiving console and stared at the computer screen forming a picture of the star Vega and its companion planets, looking like small dots on the screen. Hank typed in a code to enhance the pictures.

At 2:05 the picture changed. At first, Hank thought the computer was changing resolution formats, but as the screen's picture began to scroll, another image formed. It was not of the Vega system.

"Brian! Edward! Quickly! What do you make of this?" Hank asked.

The two scientists jumped up and raced across the lab to look at the monitor.

"It's another message from Chulos! Quick, Brian, grab the print-outs!" Edward said, pointing to the printouts from Chulos that had already been received. Brian ran to the table the scientists had been working on and picked up several sheets of paper containing the last two transmissions from the Chulosians.

Hank jumped and ran over to another console and began punching in a code Leon had loaded previously. Another terminal came on-line and the message was now scrolling onto two computer screens. Hank watched the one he had just enabled and as the message was received, it was instantly translated by Leon's image enhancer program, the symbols on the screen appearing in English.

"Brian, Edward, come take a look," Hank called to his associates.

They all studied the English translation and the complex design blueprints. Hank grabbed several documents from the table and passed them to the other scientists. They looked back and forth between the papers and the computer screens. No one noticed the door to the lab opening or Craig Williams standing in the entranceway.

***

Libby checked on Leon in the emergency room. He had a bandage around his arm and sat on the edge of a gurney. Tom Moniot was in emergency surgery for his leg and shoulder wounds.

"Hi, Leon. How are you feeling?" Libby asked, poking her head around the curtain.

"I'll be okay, Libby. They gave me six stitches and a pain killer. I guess you could say I'm lucky to be alive." Leon smiled.

"I'm alive, thanks to you, Leon. If it hadn't been for your quick thinking, we probably all would be dead and that maniac would have gotten away," Libby said.

"I'm no hero, Libby. I didn't have time to think. All I saw was that guy's gun pointed it at you. I did what anyone would have done." Leon grinned sheepishly. He didn't like being in the spotlight.

"You're my hero, Leon." Libby leaned over and kissed him on the cheek.

Leon smiled from ear to ear.

"I'm going over to the Center to check on Hank and the other scientists. I'll have one of the agents drive you home. Get some rest and I'll tell Hank that you'll see him and the others tomorrow," Libby said, turning to leave.

"Wait, Libby," Leon called. He jumped off the gurney and headed toward her. "I'm okay, honest, Libby. There's no reason for me to stay here and I sure ain't tired. Why don't I come with you to the lab? I think Hank might need my help anyway. Wait two minutes and I'll go sign the release."

Leon went over to the emergency room admitting counter and asked the nurse for the release form. As Libby waited, she walked over to one of the other agents who was at the hospital and asked him to call her if there was any change with Tom Moniot.

Leon finished signing out and left the hospital with Libby. They stopped at another all-night cafe, bought sandwiches and coffee for the scientists, and headed back to the lab.

***

Craig Williams, flanked by two security guards, stepped into the lab. Hank was the first to notice them.

"Craig! What the hell are you doing here?" Hank asked, surprised to see him there with the guards.

"What I'm doing here, Doctor Stanton, is supervising what may probably be the most historic event in human history. As director of the HST project, it's my responsibility to oversee everything that goes on here. Do you have a problem with that?" he asked pompously. He walked up to the console, looking at the documents and the images on the two computer screens.

"As of this moment, gentlemen, I am placing this entire project under the command of Lieutenant General Arthur Reynolds."

"What sort of rubbish is this? Have you lost your mind, Williams? We're scientists working on a significant discovery here! How dare you come in here and assume we'll just let you take this away. Why, I've never heard anything like this in my life!" McDaniels said. He was livid. He turned and ignored Craig and the two guards, motioning for

Devane to join him on the opposite side of the room where Hank was standing.

One of the guards in the room was Charlie, the front lobby security man, and Hank's friend. He felt very uncomfortable in the room and thought that the whole situation was more than a little strange. The other guard, one of the main gate security men, seemed to enjoy the whole ordeal. "Mister Williams, if you don't mind my asking, do we have the authority to be doing this?" Charlie asked uneasily.

"Mister Mcaffery, I would appreciate it if you would just do the job for which you are paid and not think. Leave the thinking to the men of science. Now, gentlemen, I want all the documents relating to this research, and I want them *now*." Craig began to pick up the documents from the table.

Hank came over and slapped his hand away. "Those documents belong right here and they are not leaving this lab."

"Mister Colleti, you have orders to place these people under arrest and if they resist, shoot them as traitors," Craig said, directing his attention to the other guard.

The guard stepped forward and pulled his .38 police special out of its holster and trained it on the three scientists as Craig continued collecting the documents from the tables. Charlie couldn't believe what was happening. Hank and the other scientists were stunned at the sight of the security guard with his gun pointing at them.

"Excuse me, Mister Williams. This isn't right. I'm going downstairs to call Mister Franklin, the head of security," Charlie said, starting to leave.

"Stay where you are, Mister Mcaffery, or I'll have you placed under arrest as well," Craig said. "Mister Colleti, I think you'd better relieve Mister Mcaffery of his weapon."

The other security guard made a motion for Charlie to hand over his gun.

"You can't do that!" Charlie yelled.

"Give me your piece, Charlie, or I'll shoot you where you stand," the other guard threatened.

Shaking his head in disbelief, Charlie surrendered his weapon to the other guard. What or who could have gotten to his colleague? Charlie wondered.

"Craig, what the hell's going on here? I refuse to let you treat us like a bunch of common criminals. You won't get away with this," Hank said defiantly.

"Oh, but I will get away with it," Craig said, reaching over and taking Charlie's weapon from the other guard.

"What do you plan to do, Craig? Shoot all of us?" Hank asked, slowly inching his way toward the computer console.

"Shut up, Stanton. Colleti, take these three to the conference room and wait there for me. I'll be a few minutes," Craig said, motioning to Charlie, McDaniels, and Devane.

The two scientists were reluctant to go and Charlie, although retired and in his fifties, was waiting for the right moment to jump Colleti and disarm him. He tried to catch Hank's eye before he made his move, but Hank's attention was on the computer screen and the new message coming in from Chulos.

Colleti poked Charlie in the side with his gun and said, "Get moving." He waved the pistol at the two scientists, motioning them to follow Charlie. They all began walking slowly out of the room when Hank stepped up to Craig Williams.

"Craig, you won't get away with this. You'll spend the rest of your life in prison for what you're doing. This is invaluable research material and you're taking it at gunpoint." Hank stalled for time.

"Prison? You have been trying to conceal this discovery ever since it occurred. For what purpose, Stanton? So you could bypass the Agency and take all of the credit for yourself? Prison, ha! The only person guilty of any crime here is you! Hank, you have no idea what's going on here, do you? This data is much too important to be left in the hands of a few scientists. It must be turned over to the military. You know that," Craig said with an almost conspirational tone.

"Sometimes, Craig, you act as if NASA were your own private little company. You fail to realize that this organization is owned and operated by the tax-paying people of the United States of America. This data must be turned over to the NSC. The President must be informed about this discovery. Think what this could mean to science and the entire world," Hank said.

The two scientists and the two guards stopped at the doorway of the lab to listen to the exchange between Craig and Hank just as, down the hall, Libby and the other two agents stepped out of the elevator.

"Hank, you're a fool. Do you think that we're in this science business just for the fun of it. We're in this for profit, too. If we didn't have the quality failures with the telescope, we would have lost our shirt on the project. With the COSTAR mission, we've added another 140 million dollars to the price tag. Don't you see, Hank? It's not just results I'm looking for. I have to show some monetary gain for what we're doing here. We have to fight for these programs while Congress wants to shut us down. Now enough of this chatter, I have work to do. Colleti, take those three into the conference room. Doctor Stanton and I have some personal business to complete."

The guard ushered Charlie and the two scientists into the hallway and closed the lab door behind him. As soon as they rounded a corner in the corridor, an FBI agent got the drop on Colletti and disarmed him. Libby motioned them to be quiet as she and the other agent went to the lab door. Libby looked through the glass door window and saw Craig, a gun in his right hand pointed at Hank and a bunch of papers in his left hand.

"You have a choice, Hank. You can join me and General Reynold's team, or you can be out of the picture and out of a job; the choice is yours. What's it gonna be, Hank?" Craig waited for Hank to answer.

Hank's mind raced. All of the material, including the data from McDaniels and Devane, as well as Leon's communication device would be turned over to the military and buried in secrecy. He couldn't allow that to happen, at least not before they had the chance to present their discovery to the NSC and the President.

"You'll never get away with this, Craig. We must be allowed to present these findings to the NSC," Hank stalled as he saw Libby waving her pistol in the window of the lab. Craig's back was still to the door.

"I'm sorry, but we don't have time to argue. My decision is final. As of this moment, Doctor Stanton, you are no longer employed at NASA," Craig said as he started to back towards the door.

"I don't think so, Mister Williams. I'll take that if you don't mind," Libby said, bursting into the room with the other agents behind and to the side, their weapons out and trained on Craig.

Craig was momentarily startled at the sight of a .357 magnum in Libby's hand pointed at his heart. He also saw her FBI credentials hanging around his neck.

With Craig distracted, Hank leaped at him and punched him square in the mouth. Craig, the gun, and the papers went flying.

Hank rubbed his knuckles as one of the agents put handcuffs on Craig. He grabbed him by his shirt and dragged him to his feet. "Craig Williams, you have the right to remain silent. Anything you say..." The agent took Craig Williams out of the lab, reading him his rights.

Craig screamed out, "You won't get away with this! I'm the Director of this project and I've done nothing wrong. You haven't heard the last of me. You'll see. I'll have this project back under my control in no time. Do you hear me? Take these god-damned cuffs off of me!"

"Good riddance to bad rubbish!" Brian McDaniels yelled after him.

Devane and McDaniels came back into the lab to check that everything was okay. Devane knelt to pick up the papers Craig had dropped. Hank was still massaging his knuckles.

"Well done, Hank," McDaniels said, clapping him on the back

"You certainly showed him," Devane chipped in.

Hank smiled and walked over to Libby. He was beat from all the work and excitement. "Thanks, Libby. Looks like we owe you again. The cavalry showed up in the nick of time. Well, gentlemen, I think we've had enough excitement for now. What do you say we all catch some sleep and meet here at four p.m. to decide on our course of action?"

"Good idea. Four it is," McDaniels said.

Devane nodded in agreement, and they both left the lab as Hank put the documents into a desk drawer and locked it. "Well, Libby, it's almost five in the morning. How about breakfast?"

128

"I'd love to, Hank. How about I cook?" she asked, grabbing Hank by the arm.

"How can I say no? I'm your prisoner, officer. Take me away," Hank said grinning as they left for Libby's apartment.

***

As Craig Williams was being led away from Goddard Center, General Reynolds was holding a secret meeting 2,000 feet under the hot sands of Death Valley, California. The Mine was prepared as the head-quarters and staging area for a mass invasion of aliens. Everyone who worked there had been hand-picked for his allegiance to the General and his agenda. Now, a few new employees had appeared, shape-changers in human form. The Eltorum Shayloree.

The General and his new associates were busy laying out their plans for the conquest of the planet, and their retaliation against the Chulosians for interfering.

20

Libby drove Hank to the townhouse she rented in a suburb of Maryland, about twenty minutes from Goddard Center. They pulled into the small driveway and Hank got out, ran around the car, and opened the driver's door for Libby.

"My, my," she said. "What a gentleman."

"Chivalry is alive and well," Hank said, bowing as Libby got out of the car. She grabbed him around the waist and gave him a hug.

"Is this any indication of the shape of things to come?" Hank asked, returning the hug.

"I hope so, Doctor Stanton."

She opened the door and they stepped inside the dark apartment. Libby locked the door behind them and turned to face Hank. Grabbing him around the waist, she stood on tip-toe to give him a warm, moist kiss. Hank lifted her up in a warm embrace as they stood there together in the dark.

Affectionately pushing him away, she asked, "What about breakfast?"

"Who's hungry?" Hank said. He continued to kiss her, only more passionately. For several minutes, their mouths and tongues explored each other, then Libby took him by the hand and led him off into the bedroom. She turned on the lamp and motioned for Hank to sit on the edge of the bed. She went into a walk-in closet, retrieved something on a hanger and retreated into the bathroom. "I'm going to slip into something a bit more comfortable. Make yourself at home, Hank," Libby said with a girlish smile.

Hank noticed the clock radio on the night table and tuned it to a soft music station. He heard Libby undressing in the bathroom. She was beautiful, he thought. He wondered why it had taken him so long to notice. There was something about her, a tenacity and intelligence in a very beautiful package. His desire swelled.

He took off his shoes and his tie. As much as he wanted to make love to Libby, he felt a bit awkward. He didn't want to rush her if she wasn't ready. He noticed two matching candle sticks on Libby's dresser. He got up, took one and placed it on the night table. He found a book of matches in the night stand drawer and lit the candle. He turned off the bedside lamp. The candle cast a warm, soft glow around the room as Libby opened the door to the bathroom.

"Well? What do you think, Doctor?"

Hank couldn't believe his eyes. The warmth within him grew to intense heat. Libby stood there in a short red lace negligee with matching panties.

"Libby," was all that he could say.

She walked over to the edge of the bed where he sat and knelt at his feet. She picked up each foot and slowly removed his socks. She then moved up and, caressing his neck, slowly undid the buttons on his shirt and removed it.

Libby's breasts pressed against his legs. He stroked her hair as she pushed him back onto the bed. She delicately ran her hands between his thighs until she reached the zipper to his pants. Instead of pulling it down with her fingers she lay on top of him, grasped the zipper in her teeth, and pulled it down. Hank could barely contain himself. He wanted to pull her down on top of him and take her.

Libby, however, had other ideas. She stood up and grasping each pant leg, removed his trousers. She placed them neatly on a chair and just stood there at the foot of the bed. Hank stretched out on the bed, his growing manhood straining the seams of his shorts. Libby just smiled at him. In the background a soft romantic song played. Slowly she slid a shoulder strap off, revealing a full perfect breast with a large, almost black nipple. And just as slowly, she dropped the other strap and let the negligee fall. Hank just stared at the perfection of her olive skin, full breasts, and narrow waist.

Libby bent forward and eased Hank's shorts down. This wasn't easy considering his condition, and they both giggled. At last he was free, standing proud as a lighthouse.

"Libby, come to me. I want you more than I've ever wanted anyone before in my life."

Libby stood up again and slowly eased her panties down, letting them drop to the floor. Hank could only stare at her tight, black curls forming a perfect vee. Hank clenched his fists in anticipation as Libby crawled slowly up the bed towards him, her breasts swaying gently from side-to-side. She knelt on top of him, and as she eased herself down on him, they both gasped at their mutual heat.

As Libby moved gently up and down, Hank cupped her breasts, his thumbs exploring her dark nipples, their eyes exchanging as much energy as did their bodies. Libby arched back, her breasts pointing upward, and then leaned forward to kiss Hank, her erect nipples brushing his chest.

Then Libby rolled over, pulled Hank on top of her, and they exploded simultaneously, their eyes and lips locked together. Their passion spent, they separated and fell asleep in each other's arms. The last thing Hank remembered was Libby's sweet breath on his cheek.

***

Libby woke at three in the afternoon. Her years of FBI training allowed her to program her mind to wake up as required. Her movements woke Hank and as they cuddled, his desire for Libby reawakened.

"No time for that," Libby said playfully. "Time to rise and shine. Duty calls." She pulled the covers off of him and jumped out of bed. "I'll make the coffee while you shower," she ordered with a sweet laugh.

Hank lunged to pat her on the rear, missed, and nearly fell out of bed. He got up, went off to the bathroom, and started the shower. A minute later the door opened and Libby slid in. They kissed deeply as their wet bodies clung to each other. They made love again, with Libby's back against the shower wall, her legs around Hank's waist. Hank's hands under Libby's firm, rounded buttocks moved her slowly forwards and backwards until, kissing deeply, they climaxed together.

They finished showering and dressing, and after toast and coffee, they left for Goddard Center like a married couple on their way to work.

Libby dropped Hank off at the front door to the lab. She had to go downtown to the Bureau field office to begin working on the arrest report for Craig Williams. She would be back later in the day to pick up the things in her desk. She told Hank that she would also be stopping by the hospital to see Tom Moniot.

Before she drove off, Hank leaned into the car and kissed her. He had a hard time pulling himself away as her full moist mouth and tongue responded to his.

Hank walked into the lobby and up to the podium in the center. Charlie was there as usual.

"Good afternoon, Doc," he said, a broad smile on his face. Charlie had had a good view of their farewell.

"Hi, Charlie. Everything okay?" Hank asked.

"Couldn't be better, Doc," Charlie said, passing Hank's ID badge through the employee verification unit.

"Last night was a lulu, huh, Charlie?" Hank said, walking toward the door to the lab.

"One I'll never forget. Have a good day, Doc."

Hank walked down the corridor past Craig Williams' office. Yellow FBI tape criss-crossed the door. They're going to have a field day in there, Hank thought, continuing down the hall. He passed Libby's office and stopped. He was a little sorry she wouldn't be coming back to work there. He'd miss her, but only at the office, he thought, as the memory of her eager body crossed his mind. He was falling for her and it felt good.

Hank walked around the corner and stepped through the door of the Space Science lab.

Brian McDaniels, Edward Devane, and Leon Beardsley were hard at work. Papers and electronic equipment were strewn all over the lab.

"Good afternoon, Doc. Last night was sure somethin' else, huh? That Libby, she's some woman," Leon said as he worked a wire into place with the soldering gun.

"Yeah, Leon. She sure is." Hank smiled. You don't know the half of it, he thought. "Good afternoon, everyone. What in heaven's name are you guys doing here? This place looks like a bomb went off." He walked around the table where the scientists were working.

"Hank, I must compliment you on this young man here. Leon's work on the Chulosian discovery and this communications device are nothing short of genius. Now, if we can just get permission to re-direct the Starmapper probe, we'll have a good shot at real-time communication with the Chulosians," McDaniels said, giving Leon a pat on the shoulders.

"Yes, Brian, the probe. I've been thinking about that. Leon, how's the Chulosian code breakdown coming?" Hank asked.

Leon looked up from the workbench and said simply, "It's done."

"Done? What do you mean, done?"

"It's done, Doc. We've deciphered the whole thing," Leon said.

Hank looked at the other two scientists as if he thought Leon might be joking.

"He's right, Hank," McDaniels said. "We finished it with the help of Leon's computer database. We now have the entire message and after you read what it says, I think you'll agree it's time to report this discovery to the President." He handed Hank a stack of papers containing the Chulosian translation.

Hank took the papers from Brian and sat down at a desk on the other side of the lab. He looked over them for a full hour while the others continued with their work. He picked up the phone and placed an urgent call to Dr. Michael Carter, chairman of the National Science Council and close advisor to the President.

"Doctor Carter, this is Hank Stanton at the Goddard Center. We have just finished decoding a message from another civilization about twenty-seven light years from Earth. It came through the Hubble, and it appears that our planet is in grave danger. We have been given the blueprints to build a device to protect us from it, but we must act on it urgently."

Carter was shaken and agreed to meet that evening.

Just as Hank put the phone down, Libby entered the lab looking very unhappy. "I have some bad news, gentlemen. It seems that Craig Williams has some very powerful friends in government. We couldn't hold him. He was released this morning on his own recognizance."

"Damn!" Hank said. "I guess that means he'll be resuming management of the Hubble project."

"Not exactly, Hank. He left for California an hour ago," Libby replied.

A puzzled look came over Hank. He tried to remember something Craig had said to him the night before. Something about General Reynolds and the facility at China Lake. "Then I guess we can proceed," Hank said.

"I don't see why not," Edward Devane piped in.

"Yeah. Who's gonna stop us?" Leon asked, more as a statement than as a question.

***

Later that evening, Hank met with Dr. Carter and convinced him of the necessity of speaking with the President and the full Committee. A late night, emergency meeting was set up at Camp David. As Hank and the others drove out there, they worked on their presentation to the President.

They arrived at Camp David and were greeted by Dr. Carter. They were ushered into what looked like a war room, already occupied by several other members of the NSC.

The President swept in and came straight to the point. "Doctor Stanton, can you please explain to me in layman's terms what this all means for the country and the rest of the world?

"Well, Mister President, according to the messages we've received from a planet called Chulos, in less than ten months, a pulse of deadly radiation will strike the Earth. The probability of the destruction of every living thing on the planet is very high."

"And what is your recommendation, Doctor Stanton?" the President asked.

"Well, sir, according to the messages and our calculations, if we can mobilize the resources we need, we can build what we're calling a Pulsar Fence in nine months. I know it's cutting it fine, sir."

"So, just what are these resources you will need?" the President asked.

Dr. Carter stepped in. "Sir, first we'll need to use the Starmapper probe, so we have to change its course. And in order for the communication system to work, we'll have to move up the COSTAR mission timetable. And we'll need to increase the power of the Hubble telescope by installing a special device in it. The Chulos message has provided the blueprints for what we need to communicate with the Chulosians. Doctor Stanton and his team have called it a Focal Generator."

The President listened intently as Hank and the others elaborated the enormity of the catastrophe heading towards them and the urgency of beginning a planetary defense immediately. Finally, the President stood up and addressed the scientists.

"Gentlemen, although I don't fully understand all the technical details, I think it's safe to say that we are all in agreement that something must be done, and quickly. The resources of the United States Government will be placed at your disposal. And yet that may not be enough. I suggest that we also contact scientists in Russia, Europe, Japan and the other nations, in a world alliance of scientific understanding. And to establish military support, I will order the Joint Chiefs to meet with all of you tomorrow morning. You can brief them, as you did me, of the magnitude of this emergency."

A man in a blue pin-stripe suit stood up. He was the President's Press Secretary.

"Yes, John. Do you have something to add?" the President asked.

"I do, sir. I think we've missed a very important point here. How will the public react to news of life on another planet? Sooner or later they will find out."

"I think I may have the answer, Mister President," said NASA director, Dan Silver. "Let's tell the media we've discovered life in a meteor. Microbial life, say...er...from Mars. It should be easy for the public to accept that news and, based on their reaction to life beyond our planet, we can then formulate a policy for disclosure."

Everyone laughed.

The President nodded in agreement.

21

The Pentagon briefing room was crowded with the top brass from every branch of the military. Hank and the others were seated on one side of the long oval table. Dan Silver was with representatives from NASA and JPL, and Dr. Carter headed the NSC presence.

General Frank Dawson called the meeting to order. After a short speech concerning the reason for the hastily assembled group, the General turned the meeting over to Hank.

Hank had prepared a slide presentation depicting several of the Chulosian images and a detailed drawing of the Pulsar Fence design. After speaking to the group for almost an hour, Hank opened up the floor to questions.

"Doctor Stanton, you have presented a most interesting scenario of an approaching cloud of deadly radiation. A race of benign alien fish people and the prospect of everlasting peace if we embrace this...er...what did you call it, GEE? I must admit, Doctor, that I am a bit skeptical. Perhaps it's in my nature to be distrusting, but how can we be sure that these aliens are truly who they say they are. I mean, what if this is some grand deception? Have any of you thought of that possibility?" Lieutenant General Arthur Reynolds, Commander of the US Government's Defense Analysis and Research Program was a bona fide war hero and had the respect of every military man in the room. He sat back down and studied the reactions of the other officers. He had planted the seed of doubt.

"Very good point, Arthur. Perhaps this is a possibility we should all consider," General Dawson said, addressing the room.

"But, General Dawson, the radiation cloud is coming. It has already been confirmed by three independent observatories. Why would the Chulosians lie to us? What do they have to gain by it?" Hank retorted.

"Doctor Stanton, I understand how important this discovery is to you, to all of us," General Dawson said, waving his hand around the room, "but we must proceed with caution until we can confirm for sure what the motives of these alien fish peop—"

"Dolphinoids, General. They are not fish, but dolphinoid beings," Hank cut in.

"Excuse me, Doctor Stanton. I meant the dolphinoids. According to your calculations we have very little time. I will agree to place at your disposal the resources of every department under my command. We will establish headquarters for this project at Vandenberg Air Base. I want daily updates of all activities in regard to this project. General Fisher, I am placing you in command. Have your office set up a direct link with the Joint Chiefs so that we may receive daily intel.

"Doctor Stanton, General Fisher will see to it that your team is equipped with whatever they need to get started on these towers of yours. I also understand that we need to alter the course of the Starmapper. The President has given the go ahead to do whatever is necessary to accomplish our goal, so you will work directly with the Director of NASA on that. Gentlemen, if there are no further questions, I am sure that we have a lot of work to do. Thank you, Doctor Stanton, and good luck with the COSTAR mission." General Dawson got up from the table and left the room.

Hank was elated. They had approval to alter the course of the probe and to build the Pulsar Fence towers. Now, he thought, it's time to get down to business.

He approached General Fisher and introduced himself. The General seemed very receptive and genuinely interested in everything concerning the Chulosians. General Carlton Fisher was Air Force and the commander of Vandenberg Air Base in central California. He was also a decorated hero in his own right. During the Korean and Vietnam wars, he was considered one of the best fighter pilots in the Air Force and now he commanded the country's most sophisticated air base.

He asked Hank what he would need and Hank handed him a list three pages long. "My shopping list, General."

The General looked it over carefully. "This is some list, Doctor Stanton," he said, smiling. "I'll see what I can do."

***

Hank and Leon returned to Goddard Center while McDaniels and Devane were flown out to Vandenberg to brief the team on redirecting Starmapper. NASA Director, Dan Silver, would handle the press once the operation was underway, with the cooperation of General Fisher. Hank and Leon set up the lab at Goddard from where they could direct the actual transmission of the course correction signals to the satellite.

It would take almost a week until the signals could be sent and received by the probe's on-board computers. The signals would energize the retro rockets for a controlled burn and change the trajectory of the probe. It would take another three days for the teams at Goddard, Vandenberg, and JPL to get confirmation of the burn and another day after that for the probe to slingshot out from behind Jupiter. Starmapper's original mission had been to map as much of the planet Mars as possible and relay that information back to Earth. Its powerful solar engine would allow it to function for over two years.

While Hank and Leon finalized the calculations for the course correction, McDaniels, Devane, and several other scientists at Vandenberg worked on the preliminary construction of the Pulsar Fence. General Fisher was also working with his NASA intermediaries to have all Earth-stationed telescopes direct their observation windows toward the approaching radiation pulse. The Chulosians had given the scientists the coordinates for detecting and tracking its approach. Doing so would aid them in measuring its speed and more closely predict the date of its striking Earth.

Hank and Leon spent most of their time working with other NASA engineers on developing the Chulosian Focal Generator. By order of General Fisher, only a handful of people with the necessary skills to be of service to the team were included in the project. It was classified For Eyes Only, with information released on a 'need to know' basis to only those individuals working on any particular component.

Since the Starmapper mission had been highly publicized, it was necessary to report the news of its apparent destruction to the media. However, the press release was timed to coincide with other major world events and raised hardly a stir, just as had happened with the 'microbes in the meteor' news.

Hank and Leon were successful in catapulting the satellite into a stellar gravity wave. It happened exactly the way the Chulosians said it would. They tracked its radio beacon with the telescope at Arecibo, Puerto Rico, and with the Hubble. They watched as it was picked up as if on the crest of a breaker at Oahu. It moved so fast that all they could do was track it as it coursed through the galaxy, yet the signal it sent back was as strong as if it were in Earth orbit. Hank and Leon were amazed at its success and the level of science on the planet Chulos that enabled them to do it. They knew that this would also mean a giant leap for the science of Earth.

It took almost a full day of waiting anxiously for the satellite to ride the gravity wave a distance of almost 27 light years. Hank was awed by the fact that under normal circumstances it would have taken thousands of years.

Leon checked the coordinates of the satellite with a new program he had developed for just that purpose. The Starmapper probe was much too small to be seen visually, even by the Hubble, but thanks to Chulosian technology, the radio telescope at Arecibo could communicate with it as though it was down the street. Leon had done it again, Hank boasted to everyone. They were only a few days away from placing the call.

Despite both their hectic schedules, Hank and Libby managed to arrange a few precious nights together. And to their delight, the passion between them continued to grow and deepen. Without either of them realizing it, they had fallen in love.

***

Kamal Tarn's associate had sent the last message to Earth as he and his fellow scientists of the Circle of Comastyr tracked the path of the radiation pulse. They stood around the Corbal Ring of Infinity and watched the stellar drama unfold. The Ring was like a window on the universe and it allowed them to focus on any area of space they wished, almost like tuning a television to any station.

They could see the remnants of planets that were in the wake of the massive pulse of radiation. Kamal and the others were glad that none of the planets harbored sentient life forms. As they watched the pulse engulf planet after planet, the destruction was total. Plant and animal alike were instantly incinerated in the flash fire that left the planets burnt out.

Kamal knew that the pulse would eventually dissipate, but it would be at least seven light years beyond Shoone Peltoran–3 before that would take place. By that time, the planet would at best be reduced to a burnt out cinder. Lifeless, forever. At worst, it would be millions of hunks of rock forming a new asteroid belt around the sun.

As the Chulosians stood around the ring, they received the thought-merging from the Council. Kamal was being summoned to stand in the circle again. They all knew that Kamal had defied the Circle of the Gee and thereby broken the law of the Council of Circles. He was to be banished from Chulos forever. Because he was a scientist of great knowledge, his entire Chotor made the trip to the Hall of the Circles together, except for Crayto Shueneenee. He would make one more attempt to contact Shoone Peltoran–3 and then turn himself over to the Council to stand with his brother scientist, Kamal Tarn.

***

Hank and Leon were at the Goddard Space Science Lab while McDaniels and Devane were busy setting up a comlink with the tele-scope at Vandenberg. Leon's new program was loaded and they were about to run a transmission test to the satellite to be sure that the up-link was operating properly. The scientists were gathered at both locations as Leon programmed the first message and broadcast it to the Starmapper probe.

"Everything's ready, Doc. Here goes," Leon said, as he pressed the Enter key on the computer keyboard.

"It should be received and re-broadcast in three minutes, Brian. Your receiver at Vandenberg should pick it up the same time we do," Hank said, talking into the speakerphone on the console.

The scientists were silent as they anxiously watched the clock. The seconds ticked by as the message hurtled across the galaxy to the Starmapper.

"We, the people of Earth, extend the hand of friendship to the people of Chulos."

The invisible transmission beamed across the vast, empty expanse of space and was picked up by Starmapper's antenna. The probe, now renamed the Chulos Surveyor, received the signal and its onboard computers executed Leon's new program, relaying the message back to Earth. The signal reached the Hubble telescope two minutes and twenty seven seconds later, and was beamed back to the surface. As Hank and Leon watched the monitor and listened to the speaker, the message came in. A computer-generated digital voice repeated the message for all to hear as it displayed it on the monitor. On Chulos, the message would be received as a digital picture.

"It's working!" Leon screamed. "Doc, we did it!"

"Yeah, I guess we did, Leon," Hank said proudly.

"Congratulations, gentlemen. We have just begun a new chapter in the history of communication. Leon, do you have the Chulosian symbol code translator ready to send?" Brian's voice asked from the speakerphone.

"Yes, Doctor McDaniels. Loaded and ready to fly," Leon replied.

"Then, gentlemen, I suggest we place a call to the planet Chulos and see who picks up the phone," Brian said.

Leon looked over at Hank and gave him the thumbs-up sign. Hank smiled and said to Leon, "Let's do it."

Leon typed in several computer commands that were beamed to the telescope and then carried on a departing gravity wave to the Chulos Surveyor. He inserted the disk containing the Chulosian translator into the computer's CD-ROM disk drive. It would convert the message into Chulosian symbols that Hank hoped they would understand. Leon keyed the command sequence and the message was sent. All they could do now was wait.

***

Kamal Tarn arrived at the Council Hall of the Circles of Chulos knowing he was to be exiled from his home forever. He had done what he thought was right and defended his position to the Council. There would be no more defense now. The thought-merging of the Council was over and the decree for his banishment from Chulos was sealed.

As he entered the central chamber, the members of the Circle of the Gee were already assembled. In the center of the room was a Corbal Ring, its Cotera Tunnel already visible as the swirling vortex contained the holographic image of the rock world Pelnor, the planet of exile.

"Kamal Tarn of the Circle of Comastyr, you have defied the Council of the Circles and closed your mouth to the Circle of the Gee. It is our dishonor to place the thought-merging of a great Chulosian such as yourself into the Cotera. You know the consequences that have been handed down by our forefathers. The rock world Pelnor will swallow you up and from this time forward, all merging of thought on Chulos shall be without the image of Kamal Tarn. It is therefore the order of our thoughts that you step into the vortex of Pelnor and leave Chulos forever. The circle has been opened and closed without you. It is done."

The Podor completed his thought-merging and all the Chulosians on the Council turned their backs on Kamal Tarn. They joined hands in a circle with Kamal standing outside of it. Being cast out of a circle was the ultimate dishonor because this ritual essentially made Kamal Tarn a non-person.

Two Chulosians wearing masks to cover their mouths approached Kamal and escorted him to the edge of the Corbal Ring. He stood at the ramp that led up to the center and the swirling vortex image of the rock world Pelnor.

***

"Forty-five minutes, Doc, and nothing. Maybe we should send the test transmission again. Maybe we're just hoping for the impossible," Leon said dejectedly.

"I know it's working, Leon. I have a gut feeling. We have to give them time to understand how our translator works. Don't worry. They'll answer," Hank said, walking over to Leon and placing his hands on the young man's shoulders.

"Brian, anything happening on your end?" Hank asked. He already knew the answer.

"Sorry, Hank. Nothing to report here," Brian answered.

Suddenly the entire computer console lit up. The cursor started bouncing up and down across the computer screen. Leon and Hank didn't say a word. The speakerphone was silent except for a low hum of static. The message came up on the screen. It repeated over and over: "Greetings, inhabitants of Shoone Peltoran–3. We hear you."

The message came on the screen as a group of images and symbols. Leon's translator instantly converted them into an audible response.

"Awright!" Leon yelled. He jumped up and grabbed Hank in a bear hug. "We did it! We did it!"

They heard shouts and whoops on the speakerphone as the same scenario took place out at Vandenberg.

"Shoone Peltoran–3? Hank, that must be what they call Earth!" Leon shouted. He quickly typed the new name into the database.

The message scrolled on the screen over and over and then it stopped. Leon and Hank ran back over to the monitor to check that everything was still operating properly. Then a new message came through. This time it had a face.

***

Crayto Shueneenee was amazed. He was standing before his own Ring in the house of Comastyr when the message appeared in the vortex. He opened his mouth and began to stroke his own tongue in a show of real joy and pleasure. He watched and listened as the symbols swirled in a watery matrix above him. Out of the matrix came the word images and the sounds:

"We, the people of Earth, extend the hand of friendship to the people of Chulos."

The image was suspended, as if by wires. Crayto immediately engaged in thought-merging and sent a greeting back to the Peltoran people. He knew they would receive it immediately and began thought-merging a new message. He told them of himself and Kamal Tarn and what Kamal had done on behalf of Shoone Peltoran–3.

***

Hank, Leon, and the other scientists were elated to receive the new message. They didn't understand what thought-merging was, but they all wanted to help the alien called Kamal Tarn.

"Leon, I need you to send a new message for me." Hank said.

"Sure, Doc. What do you want to say?" He asked.

Hank grabbed a notepad and pen and wrote down a short message. Then he ran out of the room and down to one of the secretary's cubicles. Hanging on the panel of one of the partitions was a picture calendar. Hank ripped off a picture and took it back to Leon.

"I got to hand it you, Doc. This says it all," Leon said, looking at the picture Hank gave him. Leon placed the paper on the desk in front of him and keyed in Hank's message. Then he placed the picture on the scanner. He energized the transmitter and the message and digital image was on its way to Chulos. Hank, with his fingers crossed in the air, said to Leon, "I hope this works. It's our only chance of saving Kamal."

He sat at the console with Leon, and again they waited for an answer.

***

Crayto received the message as Kamal was almost in the vortex. As soon as Crayto understood what the Peltorans had sent, he thought-merged with the whole planet of Chulos. The thought picture that every Chulosian received from Crayto was the image that Hank had sent to the planet along with a message. But Kamal, his mind having been denied thought-merging, had no idea what was going on.

The Council heard Crayto's call and demanded that Kamal step away from the Cotera Vortex. They re-admitted him to the thought-merge, and Kamal heard the message. "Great people of the planet Chulos, we are children lost in the sea of the universe. Kamal Tarn has given us the hope of life. Let us join our two worlds together and accept the Circle of the Gee as one family."

Crayto thought-merged the picture to every Chulosian. It was one of James D. Watt's photos of dolphins leaping from a crystal blue ocean.

Everyone on the planet Chulos stopped and thought-merged with one another.

Kamal was formally pardoned by the Council and asked to intercede on behalf of Earth. Crayto sent a new image back to Earth. It was received by Leon's translator and instantly digitized into an audible signal. It was only one word.

"Brothers."

22

Everyone was elated when they received the one-word message from Chulos. It meant the beginning of a new age of discovery. Hank and Leon couldn't keep from smiling as they danced around the lab at Goddard. Edward Devane came back on the speakerphone. "Hank! Hank! Are you there?" he asked.

"Yes, Edward, I'm here," Hank answered.

"Hank, let's not lose sight of the danger that still confronts our planet. We still have many questions about the design of the Pulsar Fence. Only the Chulosians can provide us with the answers," Edward said.

"Yes. You're right, Edward. I think it would be best if we all met with General Fisher as soon as possible to work out a plan of action."

"I agree, Hank. How soon can you and Leon come out to Vandenberg?"

"Edward, we'll be there as soon as we wrap things up here at Goddard," Hank said.

Hank thought the best course of action would be to meet with everyone at Vandenberg and work out the strategy for constructing the fence. They all concurred that contact with the Chulosians should remain a secret for the time being. Besides, the President felt he still needed more time to assess the full impact of what was happening before the public could be made aware of the news of contact with extraterrestrial life, not to mention the impending radiation storm. Hank came up with a plan that he thought would mask the real purpose for the construction of the Pulsar Fence from the media. At least temporarily. They would all meet at Vandenberg in less than two days.

* * *

Kamal Tarn and the entire membership of the Circle of Comastyr met to discuss how they would provide the necessary assistance to the rock worlders of Shoone Peltoran–3.

Bosenjoe Marluca, a respected member of the Council of Circles, suggested that Kamal Tarn and an entourage of Chulosians travel to Peltoran-3. They could provide the technology for the construction of the fence and also open the door of friendship. He felt that the wisdom of the GEE was again directing them to the people of Shoone Peltoran–3.

The GEE was the light that guided Chulos. Invisible and untouchable, it was the universal life force energy that filled their entire way of life. The Chulosians believed that the GEE was a gift that existed for the benefit of all living things in the universe. It was the energy that made it possible for all Chulosians to thought-merge. The genetics of the Chulosian race had been open to it since the time of the awakening, and although its power existed in every life form, only those that had developed thought could realize the GEE within themselves and use it in their species' evolution. Species that were unaware of it were denying themselves the greatest gift the universe could offer.

Kamal felt the awareness of the GEE in some of the rock worlders of Peltoran–3. He knew that when they learned to thought-merge, they too could enter into the great Circle of Light. The Chulosians possessed great knowledge and understanding of all living things, but Kamal knew they must be careful. It was like the old times, he thought; the time of the first awakening when some opened to the GEE but many would deny it, or try to use it to control others. And also, the darkness of the Eltorum was hanging like a cloud over Shoone Peltoran–3.

* * *

Brian McDaniels and Edward Devane returned to Cartagay Island to continue preparing for an Earth-wide comlink with Goddard. The President had secretly brought the leaders of other major governments up to speed and enlisted the aid of their best scientists. Some would help in the construction of the Pulsar Fence at Antarctic Station in the South Pole. Others would join General Fisher, who was spearheading the team that would build the North Pole section of the fence at Prudhoe Bay Air Force Station.

Hank and Leon arrived at Vandenberg to help with the construction of the pulsar towers. General Fisher had agreed with Hank's idea of masquerading the project as an atmospheric analysis test array, code-named HAARP.

Another team was assembled at the Jet Propulsion Lab. Hank assisted them in creating a new uplink to the telescope from JPL. It was painstaking work, very technical and highly classified. In order for the Pulsar Fence to work, it would require enormous electrical energy to create the pulsed microwaves that would blast into the atmosphere at hypersonic speed. As far as Hank knew, Nikola Tesla was the only human to ever conceive of such a scientific marvel. He wished that Tesla's notes still existed.

Hank and the other scientists understood the Chulosians' instructions for building the fence, but many of the design components and materials that could withstand the tremendous heat had only recently been developed. Without time to test the system, no one knew if any of this would work. They did know that completion of the Pulsar Fence would require their teams to work around the clock.

Hank and Leon discussed the construction problems at length with the other scientists. The conclusions they reached were unanimous. They must have more technical information from the Chulosians or the fence might never be completed. Hank knew what they were driving at as he thought of the logistics of the situation. The people at JPL were some of the best minds in the country: materials scientists, mathematicians, physicists, and engineers. General Fisher had assembled a team of the most competent scientists on the planet to work on the problems of construction, yet even with all of this technical know how, if they couldn't build a pulsed microwave beam that could restore the earth's ozone layer, every living thing on the planet would be destroyed.

Doctor McDaniels received data on the progression of the advancing radiation pulse on a daily basis. The other astronomical observatories that had been made aware of its existence joined General

Fisher's team of scientists. Nine months was all they had left, according to Doctor McDaniels' and Professor Devane's calculations. Several other astro-physicists concurred with their findings. General Fisher moved his team as fast as humanly possible. Hank worried that without the help of the Chulosians, they might not be finished in time.

Hank gave as much assistance to the General's team as he could and everyone agreed that it was time to contact the Chulosians again. This time they wanted to try and broadcast a live video image from Earth to Chulos. Hank wanted to know if the Chulosians were capable of interpreting a video image, possibly digitizing it and replaying it on their own planet. Doctor Michael Carter of Cornell University had been working with high gain, high data rate transmissions for the QuickStar satellite program and was invited to assist Doctor Stanton and Leon Beardsley in developing a neutron beam transmitter. They hoped that it would send the video image through the Hubble on the same gravity wave that brought the Chulosian pictographs to Earth.

They assembled the equipment they needed at Goddard and retrofitted the largest dish transmitter at the Lab. They focused the telescope on the same area of space as before where Doppler wave distortion implied the movement of gravity waves through that sector of the galaxy.

Hank and Leon used a high definition camera loaned to them by General Fisher. He said it was the next generation of development in optics and similar to the cameras used on the SR-71 Blackbird, although still in the experimental stages. Doctor Carter was able to increase the speed and clarity of the signal bandwidth for the transmission to Chulos.

The electronically recorded video images were stored on a laser disc and inserted into the system. Leon, Hank, and Doctor Carter watched closely as it was energized and transmitted to the telescope for linear send-off into the gravity wave. The signal was almost sucked into the vortex of the wave as it raced to Chulos where it was received by Kamal Tarn.

* * *

Kamal Tarn was correct in his assumption that the Peltoran people lacked the knowledge, especially of the material sciences, to complete the fence. His conclusion was one of fascination and fear. They must travel to Peltoran–3 and provide the necessary skills required to complete the Pulsar Fence, but there would be problems traveling through the Corbal Ring vortex. They would need a destination they could visualize in order to project themselves there.

Although Kamal was earnest in his desire to help the rock worlders of Shoone Peltoran–3, he was aware of the dangers of Chulosian technology falling into the hands of the Eltorum Shayloree. They were the enemies of peace and thought-merging, and they hated the Circle of the Gee and its member planets. Kamal knew that they were already on Peltoran–3 and had been there for some time. He only hoped that they would be able to finish the Pulsar Fence before the Eltorum knew the Chulosians were on the planet.

Once the fence was energized, its power would shield the planet and deny the Eltorum their shape-shifting ability, thus exposing them. They would know that the people of Chulos had taken Peltoran–3 into the Circle of Planets. The Eltorum would no longer have any influence on Earth.

* * *

Hank and the others followed the path of the transmission through the galaxy. It raced at a speed no one on Earth could measure. Using the principles of gravity wave momentum, Doctor Carter privately theorized the construction of an Earth ship with the capability of skipping through space in the same manner. He saved his notes for a later time.

23

The Chulosians decided it would be necessary to travel to Peltoran–3. They gathered in the Great Hall of the Circles and thought-merged. Kamal planned to lead a delegation of seven Chulosian scientists to assist the Peltoran people in constructing the Pulsar Fence. The Chulosian delegation was uneasy because they knew from previous travels to the Outer Rock Worlds that it could be dangerous. Kamal needed to contact the Peltoran–3 message receivers and tell them to make preparations for their arrival.

Kamal knew the Peltorans had been venturing into their planet's outer gravity sphere and could remain there for a time inside their propulsion vehicles. He knew from experience that rock worlders had a fear of physical difference. The Chulosians were very different from what the Peltoran people could imagine. This too must be considered, Kamal thought, because it would incite their prejudice of anything different. To the Chulosians, the rock worlders of Peltoran–3 all looked the same. Although Kamal had sent images of the appearance of the Chulosians, he knew that in person, the Peltoran people could be unpredictable in their actions with anything alien.

"Kamal, we are receiving a thought picture in the Corbal Ring from the Peltorans in the shape of light waves. Come and see what they have done," Crayto said.

The Chulosians gathered in a circle around the Corbal Ring. It began to resonate with a melodious tone as the vortex began to take shape. The moving image of the rock worlders appeared and many of them were amazed at the appearance of the Peltoran people. Kamal Tarn was the only one among this group of Chulosians who had been to Shoone Peltoran–3 before and had actually seen Peltoran people. They all stood together and thought-merged. As they did so, the picture from Peltoran–3 grew in clarity. It was like watching a video through a fish tank. The image was wavy in the sea-like atmosphere of

Chulos. The Chulosians were fascinated as they watched Hank Stanton offer greetings from his planet called Earth.

"My Chulosian brothers, I am Hank Stanton. I am a scientist like yourselves. We send greetings from Earth to our neighbors on Chulos. To Kamal Tarn of the Circle of Comastyr, we give thanks. And to Crayto Shueneenee, we say he is a worthy friend to all who know him. Our time grows short and the peril that is coming to our world grows closer with each Earth day. Your help is needed to complete the Pulsar Fence on our planet. Our material science is not as powerful as that of Chulos. Can you come? We believe in the power of the Circle and we wish to join with you in the center. The GEE is strong in our world, but we do not know it. It is your science and the power of the GEE that will save us. Can you come?"

The signal wavered and then it melted as if it were some kind of illusory phantom image. Kamal and the others thought-merged and decided that they must travel there as soon as possible. Crayto broke the thought-merge and they all stood and watched him as he stepped near the ring. He placed one of his own thought pictures within the Cotera Vortex and the image of the space shuttle and the telescope in Earth orbit appeared.

"Kamal, I have formed a new image for us to see. Perhaps it would be better for us to bring the Peltoran called Hank Stanton here and introduce him to our world first. He could then relay the fence construction to the people on his planet while we teach him the ways of the Circle and the power of the GEE. If this Peltoran could be brought into the Circle first, it would be safe for us to reveal the Eltorum on his world." Crayto's thoughts touched everyone present.

Kamal agreed. It was a worthy idea to bring the Peltoran to Chulos. He would be brought into the Circle of Friends and taught the ways of thought-merging. It would also help his people to accept the guidance of the Chulosians if they trusted one of their own. They would have to make preparations for the Peltoran's visit. All rock worlders were air breathers. He would not survive the water world of Chulos unless they prepared him first.

Kamal spoke with his family in the Circle of Comastyr and explained that he would step into the Cotera and bring the Peltoran to

Chulos. Kamal would touch him with the Habadasor Elnee, the power of the GEE. That way he could survive in the Chulosian liquid atmosphere.

It was decided that they would choose the Peltoran, Hank Stanton, to be the Lector Ramoth of Shoone Peltoran–3, the first Earth brother and speaker in the Council of Circles. They would send him a thought picture in order to prepare him for the journey.

***

The preparations for the Pulsar Fence continued in full swing. Hank and Leon returned to Goddard Space Flight Center and continued to coordinate efforts from there. Libby Morales took a leave of absence from the Bureau and was now providing secretarial assistance to Hank. Their love continued to deepen and they spent almost every night together.

Leon worked tirelessly on the exacting computational mathematics for the Pulsar Fence program. The scientists knew it would be almost impossible to judge from ground level what the exact moment should be for them to energize it, so they came up with the brilliant idea of letting the increase in radiation levels in the atmosphere trigger the Pulsar Fence.

Brian McDaniels called from Cartagay Island. "Hank, Brian here."

"Hello, Brian. How are things at Cartagay?"

"Not well, Hank. We have some very disturbing news. The radiation pulse has begun to broaden. It's now interfering with our reception from Chulos. We can't pick up the signal from the Chulos Surveyor satellite. We have transmitted on every frequency and received nothing back. If we can't re-establish contact, we can't complete the Pulsar Fence. It's as simple as that. We're doomed." Brian sounded frightened and angry.

"Brian, we must continue trying to regain the signal. The Chulosians may not be aware of what has happened. Leon and I will try to reroute the Hubble comlink through TDRS and perhaps increase the signal strength. It might be possible for us to penetrate the cloud just long enough to make the Chulosians aware of what has happened," Hank said.

"We'll monitor your progress from Cartagay and call you back in a few hours," Brian said, and broke the connection.

"This isn't good, Doc," Leon said. "In order for us to penetrate that radiation pulse we would need to increase the ground signal by a factor of four just to prevent distortion from our own atmosphere."

"What did you say, Leon? We would have to increase the ground signal? What if the signal wasn't boosted from the ground at all?"

"I'm sorry, Doc. I don't follow you," Leon said.

"Leon, we could boost the gain on the Hubble."

Leon's eyes opened wide as he tried to comprehend what Hank had just said. "Geez, Doc, how could we do that? The Hubble's 380 miles away, in case you forgot. That's 380 miles straight up, Doc."

"Leon, where are those Chulosian translations? The ones that show the assembly drawing for the Focal Generator," Hank asked.

They both started rummaging through the piles of documents and computer printouts.

"I got it!" Leon shouted. "This is the drawing I used to make part of the communication program."

"Leon, best estimate: how long to build one of these and harden it for space flight?" Hank's mind raced.

Leon was catching on to what Hank was thinking. "Say about a week to work up the drawings and do the math for this gyro thing in here."

Leon and Hank leaned over the table to examine the drawings.

"Another week to work up an exact bill of materials and say about three weeks to have it ready for space. That's five weeks. Then what do we do with it?" Leon asked.

"I install it in the Hubble."

Leon smiled in agreement. In his eyes, Hank had just been promoted from hero to super-hero. "Let's go for it!" he said.

24

Kamal Tarn and the other Chulosians were aware that the radiation pulse was preventing communication. They thought-merged to determine a way to penetrate the massive radiation pulse hurtling toward Peltoran–3. It was imperative that they contact the Peltorans before traveling to the planet. Special preparations would be required if the Chulosians were to go to Peltoran–3. Their first priority, though, was to regain communication with the orbiting telescope and inform the scientist Stanton that they would bring him to Chulos for a short period of time in order to acclimate him with the people and customs of Chulos.

The Chulosians tried increasing the power of the Cotera Tunnel in the Corbal Ring hoping that by speeding up the thought-merge image it would pass through the radiation undistorted. It wasn't working. Kamal and his associates then tried to go around the cloud of radiation by skipping onto another gravity wave. The result of this attempt sent their thought-merge images speeding far out of the range of Earth's primitive space and ground-based receivers.

Crayto Shueneenee suggested they create a small globe of radiation themselves and use the power of the gravity wave to plow a path through the pulse. The pulse itself, traveling at tremendous speed through the galaxy, would then catapult the globe onto Earth. They all thought-merged on the idea. Kamal Tarn agreed that it could work but suggested instead that they use the Globe of Oreth. This way he could travel in safety within the gravity wave and pass through the radiation pulse without harm.

The Globe of Oreth was one of the tools the Chulosians used to travel throughout the galaxy, carrying the Chulosian water atmosphere within the globe. It was not absolutely necessary for the Chulosians to travel this way for they could live outside their own atmosphere for extended periods of time.

They also had the ability to recreate their watery atmosphere from the molecular energy surrounding them. But the fiery radiation from the pulse was a different circumstance altogether. They could not survive going through it unprotected. It was agreed by the circle that Kamal Tarn would travel to Earth in the Globe of Oreth.

**

The work on the Chulosian Focal Generator was progressing ahead of schedule. Hank had to return to Cape Canaveral in order to brief the other shuttle astronauts on the changes in their mission. They were all briefed on the contact with the planet Chulos and the impending disaster of the radiation pulse about to strike Earth. Besides installing the Chulosian Focal Generator in the telescope, it would be necessary to complete the other elements of the COSTAR mission.

In order to boost the gain of the telescope and increase its receiving power, they would have to replace the solar panels on the Hubble with longer, more powerful components. They also had to install the tiny prescription lenses for correcting the spherical aberration of the primary mirror and remove and replace the Wide Field Planetary Camera that was the workhorse of the entire telescope.

It would require a long EVA to the telescope and Hank, although a veteran astronaut, knew that by the time they undertook the mission, the radiation levels in Earth orbit would have increased by almost ten percent. Their space suits were capable of withstanding a much higher percentage of rads in space but they could not remain in that environment for extended periods. The weak link was their space helmets. The glass composite material could only withstand limited doses of high intensity gamma rays.

Libby and Leon traveled to Kennedy Space Center; Libby to accompany Hank between briefings and Leon to work on the final construction of the Focal Generator.

Leon had to have a mock-up of the unit built so Hank and the other scientists could be certain that it would fit. The Henry River Tool and Die Company of Ormond Beach, Florida was the only company in the entire country that had the technology and resources to construct the device. Fortunately, they were within two hours drive of the Cape. Under presidential executive order, the company was instructed to cooperate with the scientists. Leon was dispatched there with the design for the Chulosian Focal Generator.

Paul Clarke, the company's president, and Rick Pflanger, the general manager, were only too happy to cooperate. They built a test bed panel and installed it in the MMU pool for Hank to practice the installation on the telescope. They had to design and build a special mount that would allow almost single-handed installation of the unit inside the space telescope.

Mark Ramius and Bill Heller would accompany Hank on the COSTAR mission as engineering technicians and safety personnel. Two other veteran astronauts would act as commander and pilot of the spacecraft.

The COSTAR mission had been widely publicized for over a year and many people in the scientific and political community were watching for its success. The entire shuttle launch was to be televised from start to finish, but General Fisher decided that the portion of the mission involving the Focal Generator installation be blacked out from the general public.

"We will cite technical problems for this segment of the mission so as not to arouse any curiosity. The cameras can be turned on when the astronauts return to the shuttle," General Fisher announced in a secret briefing.

Leon was busy supervising the finishing touches to the Focal Generator. He had designed it to fit into the telescope equipment bay that now housed the High Speed Photometer. It would be necessary to attach it between the existing device and the telescope's framework in order for the Focal Generator to be installed successfully.

The unit was designed to accelerate the broadcast radio transmissions from Earth and send them on to the Chulos Surveyor at the speed of a cosmic gravity wave. Leon wasn't exactly sure how the unit did this other than, according to the Chulosian blueprint, the signal would be caught in a type of hypersonic gyro and skipped across waves in space. He sincerely hoped it would work because they still had no contact with the planet Chulos.

***

The Space Shuttle *Columbia* was lifted onto the giant crawler in the vehicle assembly building at the Cape. It slowly made its way out to pad 39A. Hank was anxious to get the mission underway. It had been over two months since contact had been made with the Chulosians. Doctor McDaniels and Professor Devane had attempted everything possible, but the radiation pulse from the exploded star was expanding at a geometric rate and there was no way for any ground-based, Earth-originated signal to get through it. They placed all their hopes on the COSTAR mission and the installation of the Chulosian device in the Hubble telescope. To the scientists, it was the only way to reopen the lines of communication.

Out at JPL in California, work on the Pulsar Fence was nearing completion. Already many of the duplicate components had been sent to United States research stations at the North Pole and the Antarctic. Although the scientists couldn't be sure that the systems wouldn't destroy themselves once they were turned on, they went ahead with the construction anyway. They had no choice. It was either the Pulsar Fence or the end of life on Earth.

The shuttle was lifted onto the pad and preparations for launch were underway. Hank and the other astronauts underwent a final briefing from General Fisher and a host of scientists. The threat of increased gamma rays building up in the orbiting Van Allen radiation belt was becoming a reality. The launch window would be small; they had to make it.

The morning of the launch came and everything was as ready as it would ever be. The night before, he and Libby had made many promises to each other for the future which were overshadowed by the thought that there might not *be* a future. Hank's concern was heightened by reports from around the world of increased cases of severe skin cancer caused by the build-up of radiation in the atmosphere. To the scientists, it was only the beginning.

The astronauts boarded the shuttle in the early morning hours. The liquid hydrogen fuel cells were topped off and all was ready. A comlink was set up with Cartagay Island and Goddard so the mission could also be monitored from those locations.

As soon as the generator was installed, McDaniels and Devane would attempt to contact Chulos. Leon stayed at the Cape as primary controller for the generator test that would immediately follow its power-on. They all went to the NASA flight command center to watch and monitor the launch.

"...five, four, three, two, one. We have lift-off as the shuttle *Columbia* clears the tower. The COSTAR mission is underway," came the voice of NASA controller, Lee Shelgar. Everyone watched as the shuttle soared into the clouds and disappeared from view.

"Go with throttle-up," came the voice of the mission director. The shuttle slowly turned on its axis as it continued its trajectory into Earth orbit. It would take a full day for the shuttle to play catch up with the Hubble. It would take another day until they could maneuver the shuttle close enough to the 30-ton telescope in order for the astronauts to repair it.

***

"Kamal, come quickly. Look. The Peltorans have sent one of their vehicles into the orbit of their planet, and the Peltoran called Hank Stanton is aboard. Now is the time for the globe to be placed into the Cotera. We will project a gravity wave and send you to Shoone Peltoran–3. It is good that he told us of this telescope and that he travels to it. Now it will be easy to retrieve him from this Peltoran device and take him within the globe. Soon he will be on Chulos to learn the ways of the GEE. Then we shall all travel to Peltoran–3," Crayto said, mouth wide open. Kamal reached out and scratched Crayto's tongue in a gesture of gratitude.

***

The President watched the lift-off in the oval office. He was scheduled to give a news conference in 30 minutes. Several of his closest advisors were seated around the office. NASA Director, Dan Silver, stood on the other side of the room, fingering a small manila folder containing his notes on the announcement that life had been discovered on another planet. He would be introduced by the President.

"Mister President, how much time are we going to give the American people to absorb this information?" asked Ron Blasedale, the assistant press secretary.

"I don't know, Ron. I think we may have to play this one by ear. In any event, we can't wait too long. With this radiation cloud bearing down on us and the assistance the Chulosians are providing us, we won't be able to keep this from the American people—or the whole world for that matter—for very long. Dan, you haven't said very much through all of this. What do you think the effect of this announcement will be?"

"Mister President, in light of the public's attitude toward extraterrestrial life, UFOs, and the like, I think it will be received rather well. It isn't like we haven't been preparing them. Between the movies, books, and TV programs, I'd say the public has already been primed for just such an announcement. Besides, Mister President, today's news conference is only going to whet their appetite. But the revelation of a microbe fossil from Mars is a long way from dolphinoid aliens talking to us through the Hubble telescope. This is one news conference I'd rather watch on television."

"Mister President, why should it even be necessary for us to reveal the existence of these aliens at all?" General Reynolds asked. "Only a handful of people are aware of their existence and they have all been sworn to secrecy. Anyway, once this ordeal is over, is there any reason why we shouldn't return to business as usual? It's not like they're going to be dropping in on us any time soon." The General stood up and walked to the window. He waited for the President's response.

"General Reynolds may be right," the President replied. "There's no reason for us to say anything at all. If word was to leak out, and it better not, gentlemen, we could write it off as the hysteria of the UFO nuts."

They murmured agreement with the President, which was exactly the reaction General Reynolds was looking for. The Eltorum were preparing to open another portal so they could accomplish the mass infiltration of the planet without ever having to land a single craft here. With his back turned towards the group, the General smiled. It had been almost three years since he had assumed control of the Montauk Project and had it moved out to The Mine. Only a few people were even aware of the existence of the project. Sure, there had been a few leaks and speculation by the paranormal groups, but that only made it easier to hide and deny. The project was a success, allowing the creation of a dimensional portal to be established between Eltorum and Earth. The base on the Moon was only a precaution. The Eltorum were free to come and go at will.

Suddenly the President spun round to face the group. "No, gentlemen, we'll proceed as planned. So, shall we go into the East Room and get this news conference over with?" the President asked.

General Reynolds was dismayed for a moment, but thought, soon...soon.

Following the President, everyone filed out of the room. The President made his way up to the podium at the center of the room to the applause of the members of the media.

"I would like to thank all of you for coming today," the President said. "I'm sure that some of you have already heard a rumor concerning today's announcement. It seems that even the walls of the White House have ears as big as an elephant's at times."

Everyone laughed nervously.

"Allow me to introduce NASA Director, Mister Dan Silver," the President said and stepped to the side.

The Director stepped up to the podium, opened his folder, and took a deep breath. "Ladies and gentlemen of the press, we have discovered life on another planet."

25

The Space Shuttle *Columbia* continued its ascent. Propelled by its onboard engines, it accelerated to almost 17,000 miles per hour. The flight commander, Colonel Rick Fullerton, engaged the auto flight locator and the race was on to rendezvous with the Hubble Telescope. As the shuttle sped toward its orbiting target, Hank and the other astronauts prepared for their EVA and the fulfillment of the COSTAR mission.

As the shuttle streaked across the heavens in pursuit of the telescope, scientists monitoring their progress traced the shuttle's ascent from the ground. It would take almost a day and half for the shuttle to reach its destination—a geosynchronous orbit, 380 miles above the Earth. Hank and the other astronauts worked on their equipment as the shuttle closed in on its target. Hank went over every aspect of the Focal Generator installation with Ramius and Heller. They checked and double-checked their equipment and went through a dry run of the mission in the shuttle's cargo bay.

"Coming up on orbital insertion in five minutes, on my mark," came the voice of the mission commander in Houston. "Do you copy, *Columbia?*"

"That's affirmative, Houston. We copy," said Colonel Fullerton. "We're in the pike and five by five. There it is, Houston. We're in the neighborhood. We'll be in the driveway in two minutes. On my mark."

"Hank, how are things in the rear of the bus?" the Colonel asked over the shuttle's intercom.

"Everything's A-OK back here. As soon as we're in position, Mark will connect up with the arm."

Hank and the others were suited up and ready for their EVA. Each astronaut had his Manned Maneuvering Unit backpack on a stand in the shuttle's equipment bay. They checked each other's suits and life support systems. They had enough oxygen for a four-hour EVA. It would take almost an hour just to maneuver onto the telescope after it was linked up with the shuttle's remotely piloted arm. They had planned for a safety margin of one hour and had rehearsed this maneuver almost a hundred times in the pool at the Cape. Even with all the training, the astronauts were always tense when they left the relative safety of the shuttle for a free-floating EVA.

To avoid tangling with the telescope, there would be no lifelines on this exercise, and although they'd each trained with the new Safer jetpack unit on their MMU backpacks in the water pool, they had never been tested in space.

Hank, Mark, and Bill stood in the equipment bay, waiting for the signal that the cargo bay doors were fully deployed and locked in the open position.

"Gentlemen, we are in position," Colonel Fullerton said. "The doors are opened and locked. We are in a rolling apogee sequence and are coming up on a full rev. There we are. Okay, boys, we are in the driveway. We will monitor you from the flight deck and Houston's got you from the ground. Chuck will be in the equipment bay on stand-by. Happy hunting."

Chuck Bayliss, the pilot, would suit up and wait on safety watch in the equipment bay after the three astronauts cleared the cargo bay air lock.

Hank opened the shuttle's cargo bay air lock hatch. The air in the small equipment compartment made a whooshing sound as it was expelled into space. The astronauts moved as if in slow motion through the portal to the cargo area of the shuttle. The equipment and tools required for the mission were all stowed in the aft cargo containers, so the three moved through the aft of the shuttle to retrieve them.

The shuttle's huge cargo bay doors were wide open to the blackness of outer space. This was Hank's second shuttle flight and the third for Ramius and Heller. All three had been on the crew of the original shuttle mission that launched the Hubble telescope. This was almost *deja vu* for the three of them.

No one spoke as they made their way into the cargo area. The ship had rolled while approaching the telescope so the view from the cargo bay was that of deep space. Earth was below on the underside of the ship. All the astronauts could see was the total black of outer space interspersed with the twinkling of a billion stars. As they sped through space at 17,000 miles per hour, Hank looked in the direction of the planet Chulos and hoped they would be able to make contact with it after the mission was completed. As he looked out into space he also recalled that a massive pulse of death was speeding toward Earth at 186,000 miles per second.

They each went about their tasks of removing covers and hold-down straps that were on the equipment for the flight. After running through a flight checklist they confirmed that everything looked okay. Bill Heller inched his way over to the remote manipulator arm and released it from the side panel in the shuttle bay. He took the remote control panel and began pressing the buttons that energized the arm. On the end of the remote manipulator they had installed a small platform to be used by the astronauts like a cherry picker. Mark would stand on the platform while Bill hoisted him into position to hook the telescope with a tether.

They could not feel any sense of movement, even at the speed they were traveling. Having the cargo bay turned away from Earth prevented any frame of reference to gauge any motion. Hank bounce/walked to a medium-sized container that was lashed down in the back of the cargo bay. Inside the cargo crate was the Chulosian Focal Generator. He loosened the latches and lifted the cover. It floated upwards on its hinges and stayed there. Hank checked the unit and everything looked all right. He lifted it out of the cargo container and started to walk/bounce to the rear of the shuttle bay.

Mark Ramius climbed onto the remote manipulator arm's platform and slid his bulky space boots into a kind of stirrup mechanism designed to support an astronaut as he worked on a satellite while it was still clamped into the shuttle's cargo bay area. Holding the remote arm's control pad, Bill Heller energized the unit and it began to lift the astronaut out of the confines of the space shuttle. Due to the enormous bulk of the Hubble Space Telescope, it would be tethered to the shuttle during the mission. Mark Ramius rose higher and higher on the end of the manipulator arm. Its full reach was over fifty feet, but the astronauts seldom ever extended the unit to its full length.

Hank reached the end of the cargo bay as Mark Ramius was hoisted high above the shuttle. Bill Heller released the button and the robotic arm stopped its upward climb. They all turned to the starboard side of the ship as the Hubble Space Telescope came into view.

"Looks like a giant can of Coors, doesn't it," Mark Ramius said.

"Yeah, and I could use one right about now, too," Bill Heller quipped.

"Looks like one of its wings got clipped. Take a look at that solar panel, Mark," Hank said, pointing over at a twisted portion of the metal assembly attached to the cylinder of the scope.

"I see it, Hank. Looks like we're gonna be busy here for awhile," Mark said.

They scanned the body of the telescope for any other external damage that might not have shown up on the diagnostic report from Houston. Beyond the obvious damage to the solar panel, the external area of the scope looked to be in pretty good shape; the real problems were inside the cylinder.

They prepared to leave the shuttle bay and venture out into space to repair the scope. First Hank and then Bill Heller energized their jetpacks and a small burst of gas shot out from the units. They sailed across the small expanse of space between the shuttle and the scope. Hank was the first to reach the large black cylinder. As part of the unit's design there were hand- and foot-holds mounted to the interior and exterior of the Hubble. Hank grabbed hold of a handle close to the opened shutter plate near the top of the telescope. Bill Heller came up on the opposite side. Suspended 380 miles above the Earth, they free-floated in the vast expanse of outer space.

∗∗∗

Kamal Tarn and the other members of the Chulosian Circle of Comastyr stood around the platform that contained the Corbal Ring of Infinity. In the center, a huge globe was suspended, bobbing up and down in a transparent sea. Kamal walked up to the sphere and turned to face his comrades. They thought-merged about the details of the trip and then, as if on cue, they each opened their mouths wide in recognition and gratitude for the wonderful thing Kamal was about to do.

Kamal emitted a strange, high-pitched sound as he touched the edge of the sphere with his webbed hand. As if by some magic, the molecular structure of the globe seemed to become transparent. Kamal passed through the globe's exterior and as he did, he stopped the sound and it began to solidify. He stood within the sphere, suspended in a matrix of Chulosian water. They all stepped back as he thought-merged and the Cotera Tunnel began to take shape around him.

The swirling vortex of the Cotera enveloped the sphere, transforming it into some kind of holographic image of itself. Kamal, suspended within the sphere, his mouth open wide turned around in a circle and faced everyone. The globe began to emit a humming sound as the Cotera vortex absorbed the sphere and launched it into a gravity wave.

Kamal was on his way to Earth and a meeting with an unsuspecting Hank Stanton.

* * *

At Johnson Space Flight Center in Houston, a communications engineer monitoring the space transmissions flipped a switch on his console. The VOX panel light indicating open video feed from *Columbia* to the television networks went out. The rest of the world, cut off from public access to the shuttle transmissions, would not see what was about to happen out in space.

* * *

Mark Ramius had the tether line in his hand as he fed it out from a specially designed reel mounted at the end of the remote manipulator arm. It floated straight out like some Indian rope trick. Mark laughed to himself. The way things behaved in space always fascinated and amused him.

Bill Heller released his grip on the telescope's hand hold and floated over to the line. He was able to grab hold of it on the second try and as he held onto it, he gave his MMU a short burst that sent him back to the huge telescope.

Bill Heller grabbed hold of another handle and inched his way toward the center of the cylinder. There was an eyebolt mounted to the telescope and he attached the tether line to it with a special clasping mechanism. They now had hold of the Hubble by the tether and it wouldn't be going anywhere until this operation was complete. He gave the line a slight tug and was satisfied that it was good and secure.

Mark Ramius released his feet from the remote arm's stirrups and engaged his backpack for a short burst. He floated over slowly; now all three astronauts were floating in space around the cylinder of the Hubble telescope.

While Mark Ramius and Bill Heller remained suspended above the telescope, Hank made his descent inside. He held the Focal Generator in his left hand as he slowly inched his way down into the telescope.

"How's it look in there, Hank?" Mark Ramius' voice crackled through the helmet's headphones.

"I can see the aperture tangent mounting plate, and the Low Light Spectrographic Gyro. I just have to move the High Speed Photometer and the generator should fit nicely between them. I'll have to tell Leon his design fit perfectly," Hank said.

"Textbook, Hank, just like we rehearsed back at the Cape," Bill Heller said.

Hank worked slowly in the confines of the bulky space suit. He took the High Speed Photometer unit and loosened its mounting bolts. It was attached to a set of parallel rails and Hank slid it over to make room for the Chulosian Focal Generator. Hank removed the protective cover from the photometer and let it drift upwards, out of the scope.

"Mark, coming at you," Hank said, tilting his head so the fiber optic lights on his helmet played on the plastic cover as it tumbled upwards. Mark Ramius reached over into the telescope and grabbed it as it cleared the telescope's opening.

"I got it Hank. I'll just hold onto it until we go back to the shuttle," Mark said.

Hank remained suspended in the center of the telescope, just above the primary mirror. He placed the generator in its correct position and attached the electronic leads that would provide it with power. He kept his eye on the Focal Generator as it went through a series of power-up self-test routines. A green LED came on, satisfying Hank that everything was okay. He thought of Leon monitoring the device from down on the planet. "Green light on the board, gentlemen. I believe we are in business."

He looked up at the two astronauts who gave him the thumbs-up sign. Hank returned the gesture. It would work, he thought, as he scanned all of the internal instruments of the telescope making sure nothing else was amiss. Suddenly Hank exclaimed, "What the hell's going on here?"

"Hank, what's happening?" Mark Ramius called out.

"Something's happening to the primary mirror."

"In what way, Hank?" Bill Heller asked.

The two astronauts outside were now leaning over the edge of the scope, trying to focus their helmet lights down the tube. They saw the strange glow.

"Hank, what's going on in there? Do you need help?" Mark asked.

"The mirror looks like it's on fire. The primary mirror's on fire!" Hank exclaimed.

"That's impossible, Hank. It's probably just the reflection of our helmet lamps. It can't be the sun's reflection. The telescope's not in the correct position," Bill Heller said nervously.

It was impossible for sunlight to be reflected off of the primary mirror, Mark Ramius thought. We're on the nightfall side of the Earth. "Hank, Hank. We're coming in to get you."

As Mark and Bill started to go over the edge of the scope, a blinding flash of light exploded from within the telescope. Its force propelled the two astronauts back away from the cylinder of the scope. They engaged their jetpacks to move back to the telescope's opening. When they reached it, everything was calm, as though nothing had happened. They both descended into the cylinder.

"Hank! Hank! Where are you?" Mark Ramius called out.

"He's gone, Mark! Hank's gone!" Bill Heller said with disbelief.

26

Colonel Fullerton and Chuck Bayliss stood on the command deck, looking out of the starboard windows of the shuttle. "Ramius! Heller! What the hell's happening out there? Where's Hank?" the Colonel demanded.

"Hank's gone. One second he was in the scope and then there was this blinding light, and now he's gone," Mark Ramius said.

"Houston, do you copy all of this?" Colonel Fullerton asked.

"We copy, *Columbia*, but we're as much in the dark as you are. What the hell happened up there?" came the voice of the CapCom in Houston.

General Fisher, Leon, and Libby were at the Cape, listening to everything that was going on. McDaniels and Devane out at the Cartagay Receiving Station heard it all, too. What happened? they all asked, their minds numb with the shock. How could Hank just disappear without a trace from the middle of the telescope?

***

The light was blinding. Hank closed his eyes and tried to hit the wrist-pad button to activate the MMU Safer jetpack but it was too late. The light engulfed him and he realized that he was no longer inside the body of the Hubble telescope. His senses had become so disoriented he had to close his eyes for several seconds in order to reorient himself. When his head cleared and he opened his eyes, he was awestruck. Standing in front of him was a six-foot dolphin-like creature, with arms, legs, and webbed hands outstretched over his head. Its mouth was wide open and its tongue was wagging almost like a dog's.

Hank attempted to step back but realized he wasn't standing on anything solid. He turned his head from side to side in his helmet trying to make out where he was. The bulkiness of his space suit, coupled with his MMU backpack, restricted any major movement. The alien remained motionless, its hands held high and its mouth open. Hank felt the sensation of movement, like some kind of vibration all around him. He looked up and down and realized he was floating in some kind of water. He moved his hands slowly through it and noticed it gave little resistance. The watery substance moved slowly around his hand like smoke. It was then that he realized he was inside a large bubble.

"Jesus, Hank, I don't think we're in Kansas anymore," he said out loud, just to hear himself talk.

The creature moved toward Hank. Actually, it floated towards him, its dolphin mouth wide open. Hank thought that this must be a nightmare. His senses had gone haywire and he was dreaming. He looked at the keypad on his wrist in order to check the oxygen mix and the CO_2 expulsion rate. Everything was nominal so he wasn't suffering any narcosis.

"Jesus Christ! This is real," he said, as the creature floated closer. It was almost touching the glass of his helmet.

The creature's mouth was still open as its snout gently touched the glass visor of Hank's helmet. It began to speak in a sort of high pitched humming sound and stopped. Then as though someone had plugged an earphone into Hank's brain, he could hear the creature speaking to him. Hank wanted to stick a finger in his ear to clear it and make sure he was hearing what he thought he was hearing. His hand bumped the side of his helmet instead.

"Doctor Stanton, I am Kamal Tarn of the planet Chulos. I have come in friendship."

Hank couldn't believe it. It wasn't words he was hearing in his head but images that made words. He was still so disoriented that even though he stood in front of this being, he didn't realize it was the same creature he had received the picture from through the Hubble.

Then his mind cleared and he asked, "You are Kamal Tarn? How did you get here?" He looked around in the watery matrix. Outside the globe, Hank could see nothing but a dull light. Like flying through a cloud, he thought.

"Wait a minute. I don't even know where 'here' is. What's happening? One minute I was in the scope, the next thing I know, I'm in some kind of bubble. Where are the others, Mark and Bill?" Hank asked, still a bit shaken.

The being who called himself Kamal Tarn stood in front of him, its long dolphin-like mouth wide open. Hank thought, maybe he wants to eat me, or something. He tried to back up but there was no place to go.

"You are in the Sphere of Motion, the Globe of Oreth, created by the vortex of a Cotera Tunnel. We are traveling on a gravity wave to the Corbal Ring of Infinity on the planet Chulos. I have taken you from the thing you call Hubble and placed you into the Globe. Your friends are safe and unharmed. They remain at your space vehicle in orbit around your planet. Are you not pleased to see me?" Kamal thought-spoke to Hank.

He heard Kamal's words in his mind but couldn't see Kamal's mouth articulate any words. The sensation of hearing word-images in his mind was a totally new experience.

"I am very glad to meet you, Kamal Tarn of Chulos," Hank said, and thrust out his gloved hand in friendship.

Kamal took Hank's hand in his own but instead of shaking it up and down in a normal Earth-like greeting, Kamal took it and placed it on his tongue and stroked it up and down.

Hank almost pulled his hand away, thinking that perhaps this Kamal Tarn was going to bite it off. But instead he smiled as he figured that this was their way of saying hello. Kamal released his hand and Hank continued stroking the alien's tongue. He saw the creature smile, sort of, as warm thoughts of friendship filled his mind. Leon was right, I'm shaking tongue with Flipper.

Kamal placed his hand near Hank's chest. Kamal thought-merged and allowed Hank to understand what was happening. Kamal's hand began to glow as if covered in phosphorous. Hank felt a warm sensation in the center of his chest and jumped back, but the heat continued to spread throughout his body in a tingling numbness. He felt a little dizzy for a few seconds and then it passed.

"Hank Stanton, please do not be afraid. You may now remove your external shelter. The matrix will not hurt you," Kamal said, waving his hand through the watery substance that filled the globe.

Hank didn't know if he could trust this alien, but he figured he didn't have much of a choice. He undid the harness that held the MMU backpack onto his space suit and slowly it drifted below his feet to the bottom of the globe. He then looked at Kamal Tarn who seemed to be watching Hank's apparent apprehension with some amusement.

Hank slowly moved his hands to the release clamp surrounding his helmet and unclasped the two latches that secured it to the suit. As soon as the spacesuit seal was broken the watery matrix flooded the suit instantly. Hank found himself holding his breath. He could have sworn he heard the alien laugh. He was going to pass out if he didn't take a breath in the next few seconds.

Hank opened his mouth and took a deep breath. He inhaled the watery matrix material into his lungs. It felt just like air.

"I can breathe!" he said excitedly.

"Of course you can," Kamal replied in Hank's mind.

***

The two remaining astronauts returned to the shuttle's cargo bay, stepped into the air lock, closed the door, and re-pressurized the equipment bay. They removed their MMU backpacks and their spacesuits and went into the command deck area of the ship. The Hubble was still tethered to the shuttle as the two objects sped around the Earth.

Mark Ramius and Bill Heller were perplexed and worried about what had taken place outside. Did it have something to do with the Chulosians? Did they take Hank? Were these creatures really as benign as everyone had been led to believe, or were they dangerous?

The astronauts, and everyone involved in the mission on the ground, asked themselves the same question: "Where was Hank Stanton?"

***

Hank breathed normally as he eased out of his spacesuit. He found that movement within the watery Chulosian matrix offered no resistance the way water would have. He floated about the sphere trying to see beyond its confines. All he could make out was the cloud-like mist they seemed to be speeding through. He reached out and touched the side of the transparent globe, amazed to find that although he couldn't put his hand through it, it was apparently made of some kind of gelatinous substance.

"Doctor Stanton, we will be within the Corbal Ring on Chulos any moment. My brothers await our arrival." As Kamal Tarn thought-merged the word images to Hank, they were on Chulos.

The mist that had engulfed the sphere disappeared and then the sphere itself dissolved around them. Hank found himself standing in a circle on some kind of platform bordered by a railing. Kamal more or less floated out of the ring and was surrounded by other aliens like himself. Hank was amazed that not only was he on the planet Chulos, but when he glanced at his wristwatch, he realized they had traveled 27 light years in just a few minutes. He wondered what other fantastic things the technology of the Chulosians could do.

"My brothers of the Circle of Comastyr, please welcome the rock worlder, Hank Stanton." Kamal bowed as he introduced Hank.

The Chulosians who had been awaiting their return now circled Hank. They stood around him with their mouths opened wide. Hank didn't know what to do, so he looked over at Kamal Tarn, who gestured 'go ahead.' Hank proceeded to stroke the tongues of the assemblage. They all seemed to exhibit the same kind of smile as Kamal had during the journey. Heads bobbing up and down, they flooded Hank's mind with thoughts of welcome.

"Welcome to Chulos, Hank Stanton. I am Crayto Shueneenee of the Circle of Comastyr," Crayto thought-said and moved aside.

Each member of the circle greeted Hank and moved outward as they formed a large circle around him. They all presented themselves and then stepped back, the circle complete around him. They stopped and became motionless for a moment. Hank heard a humming squeal as they all began to thought-merge with the other members of the Chulosian people. Hank could hear in his head the unified voice of the entire population of Chulos welcoming him to the planet. He felt honestly at ease, but then wondered about the others on Earth. They would be in anguish trying to figure out what had happened to him. He decided to ask Kamal Tarn if it was still possible to contact Earth.

Hank tried to speak but his mouth felt like it was full of marbles. Kamal came to his side and put his webbed hand to Hank's shoulder. Hank could hear him speak, but his mouth wasn't moving. Suddenly he understood thought-merging. All he had to do was picture in his mind what he wanted to say and it was said. He wondered, how could he do this, and instantly knew: It was that warm glow when Kamal touched him.

"Kamal, it is important for me to contact my planet. They will be worried if they do not know that I am alive," Hank thought/spoke the words to Kamal.

"I know this, Hank Stanton. But first you must take a short time to see and understand Chulos. It will be easier for your people to accept us after you can explain to them who we are. I shall take you on a trip across the planet, to the Great Council of the Circles. There you will learn what you need to know before we travel back to your planet," Kamal said.

"You are coming back with me to Earth?"

"Yes. I will bring six members of the Circle of Comastyr with me. There they will assist your people in the construction of the Pulsar Fence that will protect your planet and its people. Now come, Hank Stanton. Time grows short for your world," Kamal said.

Kamal took Hank's hand and indicated for him to come by his side. The others gathered around them and they swiftly floated out of the room. The group he traveled with moved through the watery atmosphere of Chulos like a pod of Earth-like dolphins. They didn't actually swim, but kind of pulsed along, propelled by a kind of light energy that moved them all through the ocean depths of Chulos.

Hank was awestruck at the beauty of Chulos. The Chulosian world was almost more than his senses could take in. The glowing coral-like formations made the entire undersea world of Chulos light up like a shopping mall at Christmas time. The red, blue, and yellow phosphorescence was dazzling. The Chulosians were kind and friendly wherever they traveled. Hank could see that other, smaller lifeforms seemed to exist in the watery depths of Chulos. He figured that these were not fish but some kind of lower form of indigenous life. Still, Hank thought they were beautiful.

As they traveled across the planet, Hank saw towering cities of coral and crystal-like pathways stretching out further than he could see. It amazed Hank that they seemed to be many thousands of feet below the Chulosian watery surface and yet he had complete freedom of movement. This was a startlingly different and wondrous place. He hoped others from Earth would someday have the opportunity to see this fantastic world.

He thought of Libby and how he felt about her. He smiled, thinking it was a great place for a honeymoon, and then looked around to see if the Chulosians had overheard his private thoughts. Kamal responded by telling him that they had, but that Hank would soon learn to join or leave the thought-merge at will. Kamal reminded him that Chulosians have no secrets from one another.

They finally arrived at the Great Hall of the Circles, a towering structure. Hank thought its peak must reach upwards of five thousand feet or more. They passed through a gate that was actually some kind of glowing ring. Hank saw many Chulosians lining the crystal pathway, everyone with mouths opened in the customary Chulosian greeting.

Hank, Kamal, and their entourage entered into a giant circular room. In the center, Hank noticed a semi-circular platform suspended about ten feet above the crystal-like floor. Standing on the platform were seven Chulosians. They looked older and more regal than Kamal and the others. Probably the elders of Chulos, Hank thought. Kamal confirmed this.

"Welcome, rock worlder from the planet Shoone Peltoran–3. We are the Council of Chulos and you stand before the Circle of the Gee, the life watchers of Chulos and the guiders of the outer worlds. We wish to bring Peltoran–3 into the Great Circle. Kamal has told us that many of your people are ready to join. We did not believe him. You are here as a representative of your world. Are you prepared to make the

Crikodynee of Karmosh? If you are, then we will know that you are true, and Peltoran–3 will be welcome."

As the elder Chulosian thought/spoke, Hank didn't have the foggiest idea what he was talking about.

Suddenly he began to hear that humming sound again. The Chulosians were thought-merging. It felt like a thousand hands were stroking his head as the collective thoughts of the Circle of the Gee searched Hank's mind for his true inner self. It was a comfortable and peaceful feeling, as they probed his deepest, innermost thoughts. They spoke to him in his mind and he felt as if everything was going to be okay. Then it abruptly stopped. Kamal stepped up to Hank and before he knew what was happening, Kamal pulled open his shirt.

The Council elder held out his hand and Hank saw it glow the same way that Kamal's had, only much brighter. A piercing light flashed and touched Hank in the center of his chest. It felt cold, and a chill went through him as a dormant gene was awakened in every cell of his body. It was painless and was over in an instant. Hank looked down at his chest and saw a brownish mark directly over his heart.

Kamal Tarn thought-merged with Hank and poured eons of wisdom of the GEE into Hank's mind. Hank gasped as he suddenly realized the value of the great gift he had just been given.

The Council Chamber grew quiet and none of the Chulosians made a move. Suddenly, the members of the Council began humming. It soon spread to the others gathered in the Chamber. They each came and stood before Hank with opened mouths. Hank stroked each one's tongue as they passed before him. Kamal Tarn came up to Hank last. After Hank stroked his tongue, he said to him, "Come, my friend, we must call Earth."

Kamal went with Hank and the other members of the Circle of Comastyr out of the Council Chamber. At the entrance to the great hall was a globe like the one in which Hank and Kamal had traveled to Chulos. They all circled around it and it began to grow in size until it engulfed them all. Hank thought that just a few minutes ago he would have been amazed at this, but now it felt so normal and natural.

"We must travel to my home city, Hank. We will be there now." As soon as Kamal thought-spoke the words, they were there.

Hank wanted to learn more about these high-speed globes and how they worked. As soon as he thought this, Kamal Tarn filled his mind with an understanding so that Hank just seemed to know.

They entered the House of the Circle of Comastyr. In their Hall of Science was the Corbal Ring that Hank and Kamal had arrived in. Kamal stepped up to the railing surrounding the ring and began to thought-merge. Hank saw a small tornado-like disturbance begin to form in the center of the Corbal Ring. Then the Earth appeared, actually a holographic image of the planet. It grew in size and clearer in view as if it were being brought into focus by some kind of lens. He saw the space shuttle in orbit and the Hubble telescope still tethered to it by a line.

Kamal approached Hank and said, "Come, Hank. We are the voice in the mirror."

27

B rian McDaniels and Edward Devane were in the telemetry room at the Cartgay station. It was almost 2:00 in the morning. Hank had been missing now for several hours. Knowing the capabilities of the Chulosians, they had a hunch that his disappearance was not some weird accident but was planned by the beings of Chulos. Nevertheless, they had some concerns for the reason behind what they considered a kind of 'space-napping.' They stared anxiously at the blank monitor tuned to the new high-gain antenna and the Chulosian Focal Generator Hank had installed on the telescope.

***

Hank had learned how to control his thought-merging and how to sense when someone wanted to thought-merge with him. The next step in his education came when Kamal Tarn thought-merged with Hank and asked him to think the message to the telescope and pass it through the cloud of radiation to be captured by the new generator on the Hubble. The Earth people that were listening would hear his message.

Hank closed his eyes and imagined the Earth, Libby, Leon, and the scientists at Cartagay. He began to speak in his mind as though he were talking into a microphone. "This is Doctor Hank Stanton. Can you hear me?" The words resonated in his mind. He waited for a reply. Nothing. He looked at Kamal Tarn for help.

"Wait, my friend. The images of your thoughts will be heard. In a moment they will speak," Kamal said.

Hank spoke the same words again in his mind. The swirling vortex of the Cotera Tunnel in the Corbal Ring intensified and changed colors. Then Hank heard it. At first it was a faint whisper but continued to get louder and louder until Hank could make out the voice of

Brian McDaniels. The scientist from Cartagay Island sounded as though he was talking in the room.

"Hank, Hank, is that you? Where are you? What the hell is going on? Are you all right?" Brian spoke into the audio transmitter that broadcast through the Hubble telescope.

Hank smiled as the Chulosians' bodies kept changing colors and faint halos lit up around each of them. He hadn't noticed it before and wondered why. He smiled as Kamal instantly dropped the answer in his mind.

Hank's thoughts answered Brian. "I'm on Chulos. It is a magnificent planet. More wondrous than anything our science could dream of. It is a planet submerged beneath a beautiful clear ocean. I am with my counterpart here, Kamal Tarn. He is responsible for everything that has happened. Please relay a message to the Cape and tell everyone that I am fine. Please speak to Libby and let her know that I am okay. I have learned many things in my short stay here. The Chulosians are a wonderful and benevolent race of beings. They have much to teach us, and we have much to learn.

"Pass the word on to General Fisher that we will come to Earth at 9:00 a.m. eastern time tomorrow. I will arrive with seven Chulosian scientists. We will be in *Columbia's* cargo bay. Tell them to release the telescope and close the cargo doors and pressurize the bay. Once we are on the shuttle we will land at Vandenberg. Tell the General to have the Lunar Receiving Lab on hand at the base. The Chulosians will need to stay within it for a short time before they can venture into our atmosphere." It was working. This just keeps getting better, Hank thought.

"Hank, we're glad you're okay. The Chulosian world sounds wonderful. We look forward to meeting Kamal Tarn and his fellow Chulosians. I don't understand how you're going to be in the shuttle, but I will relay the message as soon as we are through. I must tell you that the radiation cloud is getting larger and is accelerating. It will be here in less than two weeks.

"The Pulsar Fence at the North Pole is complete but the Antarctic site is not finished yet. We still don't know how to tune them and synchronize the signals. I hope that the Chulosians aren't coming here to perish with us," Brian said, concern in his voice.

"Don't worry, Brian. Tell General Fisher that we will be inspecting the sites and any adjustments that are found to be necessary will be completed then. Everything will be okay, Brian. Now get on the line to General Fisher. I will speak to you again when we arrive on the shuttle." Hank's thoughts were instantly transmitted across trillions of miles. He concluded his thought-merge and the Cotera vortex began to shrink in size until it was gone, along with the holographic image of Earth.

"Come, Hank Stanton. We will visit a special place and then you shall feast on the food of Chulos," Kamal said, and they left for the central room of the Circle of Comastyr.

Hank was a little apprehensive about dining with a bunch of dolphin-like aliens. He thought-merged his concern to Kamal and was assured that their food would be to his liking, so it was no surprise that when they arrived at the home of Kamal Tarn, a sumptuous feast of delicious vegetarian delicacies awaited them.

"This is Taymal Kamashee. She is my life partner. We share all things and are equal in our thought-merging. Taymal is an explorer from the Circle of Hofellowdwyngee. They are the discoverers of the plant worlds of the Malorum galaxy. We are traders with them and all of the outer worlds of Malorum. Soon we will trade with Shoone Peltoran–3 as well. Eat, Hank Stanton. Tomorrow we shall change your world forever," Kamal said.

***

As Hank was being treated to a sumptuous feast on Chulos, back on Earth, Brian McDaniels and Edward Devane were ecstatic. Hank was alive and on another planet, the first human to step foot on an alien world beyond Earth's solar system. It was something for the history books, they thought.

Brian called up the Cape and asked for General Fisher. "That's correct, General. Tomorrow at 9:00 a.m. Eastern time…that's what Hank said…I don't know how they're going to do it, but if Hank says

they'll be on the shuttle we'd better start making preparations now."
Brian ended the phone call with the afterthought. "And could you
please tell Ms. Morales that Hank is okay?"

"Certainly, Doctor McDaniels. I would like you and Professor
Devane to be at Vandenberg when they arrive. I'm dispatching an Air
Force jet to Cartagay at once to pick you both up and fly you immediately to the base in California. I will meet you there. I want to monitor
the shuttle from the Cape so as soon as I'm sure everything is secure
here, I'll fly out there. Have a good flight," the General said.

McDaniels and Devane began preparing to leave the island at once.
They gathered their instruments and notes and made calls to both
polar sites of the Pulsar Fences. The Air Force jet arrived on the island
an hour after the General called. It would be a twelve hour flight to
Vandenberg.

***

Hank was enjoying his visit to Chulos. He was shown many sights
and wonders not only of the planet itself, but of the culture of the
Chulosians as well. Hank thought the most fascinating aspect of
Chulosian society was their all-encompassing belief in the power called
the GEE.

As Kamal Tarn explained through mental pictures, Hank was surprised to learn that the Chulosians had been to Earth many times
before, and even more surprised when he learned why. Kamal told
him there was once a great Chulosian civilization on the planet Mars
over 100 million years before Earth was inhabited. A great cataclysm
forced them to leave Mars and some of them had settled on Earth,
adapting well to the planet's oceans.

Hank learned that these early settlers also had the power of the
GEE. The Chulosian race was as old as time itself and from their home
planet they had settled throughout the universe, but wherever they
went, the Chulosians remained in alignment with the GEE. It gave
them the power to thought-merge and the ability to travel at almost
the speed of thought anywhere in the universe. As Kamal explained,
the GEE was life itself.

Hank began to realize that the Chulosians were true spiritual be-ings of light. There was so much of Earth's history that was tied to them. Hank wondered whether the people of Earth would accept these wonderful beings, or whether they would fear their power and turn against them.

Kamal sensed Hank's apprehension. "Hank Stanton, I understand your fear. Your people reside in the darkness of ignorance. The time of the 'awakening' for your world is now. Our family placed this trigger in the genetic coding of your people many thousands of your years ago. The GEE exists in you, but is dormant in most. When the time is right, your people will hear the tone of light and the power of the GEE will open in all of them. You, Hank Stanton, are the first Lector, the first of your people in thousands of years to receive this great gift of opening."

His time on Chulos was over, and he, Kamal Tarn, and the other Chulosians entered the Corbal Ring. For the first time, Hank joined in when Kamal and the others thought-merged. The Cotera vortex appeared and around it a sphere. They all stood in a circle as the large transparent Globe of Oreth moved above them and around them. They had passed through its spherical surface and were now within the bubble. In a moment they were in the vortex and everything outside turned a misty white color.

They were on their way to Earth.

28

Mark Ramius and Bill Heller were back in the shuttle's equipment bay to complete the repair of the telescope before Hank and the Chulosians arrived. They had to replace the solar panel array and electronically realign the corrective lens pack they would install on the primary mirror assembly. They anticipated a three-hour EVA max. The shuttle's bay doors were still open as they cleared the air lock and closed it behind them. The Hubble was still tethered to *Columbia* as they coasted in orbit. They retrieved the lens pack assembly and made their way to the rear of the cargo area. Mark climbed onto the remote manipulator as Bill picked up the remote control box.

Mark was lifted towards the telescope and when the arm was fully extended, he eased his feet out of the stirrups on the small platform. He touched the keypad button on his wrist and the MMU jetpack propelled him to the top of the telescope. Bill grabbed the panel array and moved slowly to the other side of the long black cylinder. Mark went down inside the scope and after almost an hour, successfully installed the corrective lens unit on the primary mirror assembly of the scope. Outside, Bill Heller had disengaged the scope's broken, twisted solar panel and reconnected the new unit.

Mark emerged at about the same time Bill finished. They disengaged the tether connecting the scope and the shuttle. Mark then used his jetpack to slowly ease his way back to the manipulator platform as Bill moved back inside the shuttle bay. Mark energized the manipulator arm and it retracted into the cargo area. As it came to rest, Mark stepped off and they both secured the unit in its holding clamps.

"Well, I'm glad that's done," Mark said over their intercom.

"I'll feel a lot better when we get this gear back inside and get those cargo doors down and locked," Bill said.

They entered the hatch that led to the equipment bay and began stowing their equipment.

Once the air lock was engaged, the shuttle's cargo bay doors slowly closed and locked. After stowing their spacesuits and MMUs, Bill and Mark went back into the cabin. It was 4:00 a.m. Hank and the Chulosians were due in five hours.

***

General Fisher, Leon Beardsley, and Libby Morales were all on the same military flight to Vandenberg Air Base. The General had already dispatched orders to the base to prepare accommodation for the Chulosians according to Doctor Stanton's instructions. The old Lunar Receiving Lab was resurrected from storage at the Cape and shipped to the air base in California. It was undergoing emergency refurbishment so it would be ready by the time *Columbia* landed.

Leon and Libby were excited to be going, Leon to finally meet the Chulosians, and Libby to see Hank. She missed him.

The President and the Joint Chiefs had been notified of the arrival time of the Chulosians. They would all be there to greet the visitors from another world, including General Reynolds who had his own greeting planned for the Chulosians. He was going to leak to the press what was about to take place on a landing strip in California.

Due to the nature of the mission and the Chulosians being on board the shuttle, *Columbia* would land at Vandenberg rather than Edwards, and the President had ordered that the base be declared off-limits to non-essential personnel until further notice. General Fisher had an entire squad of Air Force military police standing by to enforce the off-limits order. The press was up in arms. Normally they were on hand for shuttle landings and wanted to know what was different about this one. They camped outside the entrance to the base, waiting for the shuttle to land.

***

The astronauts were awakened from their rest period at 8:00 a.m. to make final preparations for the arrival of Hank and the alien contingent from Chulos. They had slept fitfully while the shuttle careened in orbit around the Earth.

Mark went into the equipment bay and suited up. He wore only his life support backpack unit because he did not intend to leave the ship. Mark peered through the equipment bay hatch into the lighted cargo hold, checking his watch as the minutes ticked away towards nine o'clock.

It happened suddenly and without warning, like the flash going off on a camera, as the shuttle's cargo bay filled with a brilliant white light. He pressed the face mask of his helmet against the portal. He couldn't believe his eyes.

It seemed to Hank that they had just entered the sphere of motion, and the next thing he knew, the transparent globe nestled on the cargo deck of *Columbia*. The Chulosians remained still as they thought-merged. As Hank would learn later, they were examining the environment in the cargo bay. The cargo hold was pressurized so Hank would not need his space helmet. He was about to remove it when he thought it would probably be wiser to talk to his fellow astronauts first.

Hank saw Mark peering through the equipment bay hatch window. Hank waved and gave him the thumbs up sign. Mark smiled and returned the gesture. Hank was almost home and it really felt great.

"Hank, old buddy, am I glad to see you," Mark said through the headphones in his helmet.

"Not as glad as I am to see you, my friend," Hank replied. "How's the pressure in the cargo bay?"

"Right on the money, Hank. Welcome back," Bill Heller answered from the command cabin.

The President and his group were patched into the shuttle's communications by a satellite uplink. As the video came on, the President addressed them. "Doctor Stanton, this is President Howell. Congratulations. I hope that everything has gone well. How are our friends?"

"Just fine, Mister President," Hank answered.

"Doctor Stanton, I wonder if you could tell them that we are all looking forward to a long and prosperous friendship with our Chulosian neighbors."

Just like a politician, Hank thought. "We'll be touching down shortly, Mister President. You can tell the Chulosians yourself, sir. I'm sure they'll be glad to know that." He was glad for the news blackout or this could turn into a political circus.

"We'll see you on the ground, gentlemen. Happy landings," the President said.

The comlink was broken and everyone in the shuttle cabin breathed a sigh of relief. The Chulosians seemed oblivious to the verbal exchange and were busy thought-merging amongst themselves.

Hank looked over towards Mark and asked, "What's our ETA at Vandenberg?"

"We're making our last orbital pass now, Hank, and then we'll start our descent. ETA in about four hours from now. That should put us down at Vandenberg around 1:00 p.m. Eastern."

Hank turned and thought-merged with Kamal and the others. "When would it be possible," he asked them, "for you to dissolve the sphere and enter the shuttle through the equipment bay opening?"

"We can enter at any time. We do not need additional time to acclimatize ourselves to your oxygen atmosphere."

As Kamal was thought-merging with Hank, the Globe of Oreth dissolved and was gone. They stood in the cargo bay waiting to enter the shuttle.

"Mark, if you could open the hatch I think we would all like to get settled in the command cabin," Hank said.

Mark Ramius undid the door latch and swung it out into the cargo bay. He watched as the transparent bubble that surrounded Hank and the Chulosians dissipated in a kind of mist. They all stood there for a moment staring at each other and then Hank began to walk towards the door.

The Chulosians followed Hank and stepped through the hatchway. As they passed Mark Ramius, he stood open-mouthed in amazement watching this group of seven dolphinoid creatures file by him like some tour group in a museum. They, of course, took his open mouth as a greeting.

As soon as they were inside and through the airlock door that led to the command cabin, Mark closed and secured the door to the cargo bay. He removed his pressure suit and quickly went through into the cabin following the group. He secured the door behind him..

There they were: the five members of the shuttle crew and the seven Chulosians. Hank thought it was going to be a crowded ride home. He stepped up to the front of the cabin and took a pair of headphones and put them on. He asked to be patched back through to Vandenberg.

"Hello, General Fisher, Hank Stanton here. What's the current position of the radiation cloud and its estimated arrival time in Earth's atmosphere?"

"The latest estimates from our stations at Palomar and Ankara put the pulse approximately three days from our atmosphere. The full force of the pulse should follow about nine hours after its initial impact. The Pulsar Fence installations at both the North and South Poles should be completed by tomorrow, but we have not yet conducted a full system test. Doctor McDaniels still has some doubts as to its effectiveness, but at this late date I don't see how we have much choice," General Fisher said.

"General, the Chulosians wish to inspect both locations immediately upon landing."

"Hank, that's impossible. It will take hours to get the Chulosian delegation to both poles."

"General, the Chulosians have brought their own transportation. They should be able to inspect both sites by evening with no trouble."

"Very well, Doctor Stanton. By the way, Doctor McDaniels and Professor Devane should be touching down here within the hour. I believe they would like to join your party on the inspection tour. They'll be waiting here upon your arrival. Also, Doctor, the Lunar Lab has been refurbished and is on the runway standing by. If you could have the Chulosians wait in the shuttle, we are going to have it towed to hangar C5A. Once inside, we'll load the Lunar Lab into the cargo bay and they can enter it from the safety of the shuttle," the General said.

Hank spent the next two hours acquainting the Chulosians with the other astronauts on board the shuttle. He demonstrated the tongue-stroking greeting and explained to Kamal that the custom was strange to rock worlders, and that he would need to explain it to everyone they met.

When it came time for reentry the astronauts aided the Chulosians in getting strapped in for the flight back to Earth. Hank observed that Kamal and the others seemed fascinated by the electro-mechanical instrumentation on board the spacecraft. They constantly thought-merged about everything they saw.

The Chulosians seemed to enjoy the ride. It wasn't the way they were normally used to traveling, Hank thought, as he watched them try to crane up and see out of the shuttle's command cabin windows.

They touched down at Vandenberg at 12:57 p.m. in a textbook landing. Outside, a circus atmosphere of politicians and military personnel awaited the Chulosians along with two members of the military press corps who were allowed access to the base by General Reynolds.

General Fisher came on the radio and told everyone to sit tight. As soon as they had engaged the tractor on the shuttle's nose wheel, they would be towed to the hangar. They felt the nudge of the tractor's tow bar connecting with the wheel, and they were pulled slowly down the runway. Looking out of the cabin window, Hank saw Libby, Leon, and General Fisher following alongside in an open top military vehicle. Hank waved but he didn't know whether she'd seen him. To Hank, she looked more beautiful than ever, with her hair blowing in the wind.

The tractor pulled them inside hangar C5A and the doors began to close behind them. They stopped just inside the huge building and a technician called on the radio asking for the shuttle's cargo doors to be deployed. Bill Heller entered a series of codes into an overhead computer panel and they heard the hydraulic whine of the doors opening outwards from the cargo bay. Mark Ramius went into the air lock of the equipment bay and into the now open cargo area.

The Lunar Receiving Lab was suspended overhead on a crane. An Air Force technician motioned him to guide the lab into the bay. The crane operator wore a pair of headphones so Mark opened a small compartment in the wall of the shuttle bay and removed a pair of headphones. They often used them at Kennedy Space Center in the vehicle assembly building when they hoisted heavy payloads on board.

Mark directed the crane operator to position the lab in the cargo area. When it made contact with the deck, it was hardly felt. We could use this guy out at Kennedy, Mark thought, as he secured the lab.

General Fisher had decided it would be best to just leave the Lunar Receiving lab in the shuttle's cargo bay with the cargo doors closed. That way they could have access to the Chulosians and vice versa through the equipment bay doors. It would also allow them to provide better security.

Mark informed Bill Heller that the Lab was down and secure. Bill punched another set of codes into the computer and the cargo doors closed and locked. Hank told Kamal that the container was aboard and that they could go inside whenever they wanted. The Chulosians thought-merged and then Kamal informed Hank that they would use it now. He led them through the equipment bay to the cargo bay and stopped dead: the bay was full of Chulosian water. Hank smiled when he saw how the water filled the bay but didn't spill out when he opened the door. It held there like a transparent wall. How do they do that? he wondered.

Kamal instantly supplied the answer as he and the other Chulosians entered the wall of water and went into the Lunar Receiving Lab. Hank closed the door behind them.

It amazed Hank how quickly the Chulosians adapted and grasped different concepts and devices. He thought they would probably be able to fly the shuttle just by looking at the gauges, but then realized that to the Chulosians the shuttle was as primitive a vehicle as a Roman chariot would be to us. Hank hoped that they would learn much from these marvelous beings, little realizing that the Chulosians' gift to him had given him access to all that they knew.

The outer hatch to the shuttle opened and the President and General Fisher walked through the door. The President walked over to Hank, who was still wearing part of his spacesuit, and gave him a big bear hug. "You deserve the gratitude of the entire world, Doctor Stanton. Now let's go meet these Chulosian fellas."

29

Kamal and the other Chulosians entered the Lunar Receiving Lab through the front door. They walked into the center of the long rectangular room and all seven of them began to move around in a circle. As they did, the watery matrix that had formed in the shuttle bay earlier began to swirl like a tornado. The astronauts crowded around the small doorway to the cargo area and watched the phenomenon.

They thought they heard a humming sound as the vortex of water swirled faster and faster until it completely disappeared. Hank looked around the cargo bay expecting it to be soaked with the Chulosian water, but it was completely dry.

The President had elected to wait outside with the other members of the Joint Chiefs and selected politicians. He wanted to present the Chulosians with an official welcome to planet Earth.

General Fisher stepped through the doorway and into the shuttle bay as the others followed. At the same moment, Kamal and the other Chulosians came out of the Lunar Lab. Everyone stopped and the two groups stared at each other.

The Chulosians were the first to move. The General's group watched as the Chulosians began to circle around them. Everyone but Hank was a little uneasy at this alien display. The circling Chulosians were humming something and then they stopped to face the group, their mouths wide open and their webbed hands raised in the air.

"Follow my lead, gentlemen. Do exactly as I do," Hank said.

Everyone watched as Hank walked among the Chulosians, scratching their tongues, after which each Chulosian would take a step back and bow. Hank then introduced General Fisher, who repeated the greeting following Hank's coaching. Again, each Chulosian bowed after his tongue was stroked.

Hank introduced McDaniels, Devane, Leon, and Libby, who were all crowded into the cabin at this point. The Chulosians seemed to take to Libby because they kept bowing to her. She blushed and was flattered by the show of affection. They were doing this out of respect for Hank since they had already learned through thought-merging that she would be his life partner.

Leon also caused a stir because of his skin color and, like a chameleon, each Chulosian changed skin color to match. Leon was fascinated with them and couldn't stop staring. One of the delegation touched his face and began changing colors. Leon couldn't help but laugh. "Hey, whad'ya know? The Chulosians are brothers under those flippers," he said.

The other Chulosians began touching Leon's face and hands. They all began glowing and changing colors like some biological light show. Everyone laughed.

Hank explained that this was another example of the Chulosians expressing friendship. "They can sense and read our feelings. If we exhibit feelings of wonder, or affection, or peace, this is what they do. I saw that often on their own planet."

Hank and the others watched as Leon walked over to Crayto Shueneenee. As he approached, Leon opened his own mouth and stuck out his tongue. The aliens all stopped and turned toward each other. Hank sensed a very short thought-merge as Crayto moved in front of Leon, and with webbed fingers lightly stroked Leon's tongue. This was the catalyst for the Chulosians to relax. They moved among the humans and stroked the tongue of each of them. Hank thought it was a wild sight.

The greetings completed, Hank introduced Kamal Tarn as the delegation leader and then introduced the other Chulosians as members of the Circle of Comastyr. While they were being introduced, the Chulosians continued to thought-merge among themselves.

The General asked Kamal Tarn if his delegation would be able to withstand our atmosphere. Kamal said that it would have no affect on them. Everyone except Hank was taken aback at their first experience of hearing Kamal's thoughts in their mind. "I'll explain later," Hank reassured them.

"Are we ready to meet the President?" the General asked, leading the way to the shuttle's exit.

Nodding in assent, the others followed, leaving the shuttle down a portable stairway.

Inside the hangar, a small podium had been set up for the President and he stood behind it. The hangar was filled with military personnel, scientists, and politicians. Two military photographers had their video equipment running as they were all ushered before the podium. The President began to speak.

"Ladies and gentlemen, today marks the beginning of a new era in the history of mankind. We can no longer consider ourselves Americans, or any other nationality. We are now citizens of planet Earth. I welcome our Chulosian neighbors with the open arms of cooperation, peace, and friendship."

Hank watched the Chulosians as the President addressed the group. They were busy thought-merging but Hank sensed that something was wrong and tapped into the merge. The Chulosians were concerned that all the pomp and ceremony was delaying their mission.

Kamal moved to the middle of the assembled group and thought-spoke in perfect English. Everyone heard him even though his mouth never moved.

"Thank you for this generous welcome to your planet Earth. We have come here for two reasons. First, to assist you in completing the Pulsar Fence and save your planet from the approaching storm, and second so that we may establish a friendship between our two worlds and share with you the knowledge and power of the GEE. Our time here is short and we must inspect the Pulsar Fence with Hank Stanton and his friends. One group will travel to your North Pole and the other to your South Pole. We will make corrections as required." Kamal stepped back into the circle of Chulosians.

Everyone was puzzled. They had all heard the Chulosian's words in their minds, but no one had heard a sound. Still confused, the President left the podium to meet with the Chulosian delegation. Hank instructed him in the proper method of greeting and everyone watched with amusement as the most powerful man on the planet stroked the tongues of the visitors.

General Fisher approached and asked Hank if they were ready to go. "A vehicle is being brought to the shuttle for transportation to the runway where we have jets standing by to take your group to the polar sites."

The President excused himself and, with his entourage, left the hangar.

Hank addressed the group. "May I have your attention please? General Fisher, it won't be necessary for the Chulosians to use any conventional means of Earth transport. They have brought their own. It is called the Globe of Oreth. We will form into two groups. Those traveling to the South Pole will go with Doctor McDaniels and Crayto here. The others will join me and Kamal Tarn as we go to the North Pole. We have thirty-six hours to complete the inspection and return here to Vandenberg. The Chulosians will be able to communicate by thought-merging. We of course will have to use radios. A special satellite uplink has been established so that we will be in constant communication at all times. Are there any questions?"

"Doctor Stanton, since we have not been able to test these structures, how can we be sure that they will work as designed? And what about the overheating problem we reported? Will this pose a threat to their success?" Edward Devane asked.

"The Chulosians believe that any adjustments required can be done at the sites. All I can say, gentlemen, is that we followed the designs to the best of our ability. The Chulosians must think we're capable or they wouldn't have risked their own lives by coming here. Anyway, at this point in time, I don't see that we have much choice. So if we're all in agreement, let's move out."

***

The radiation pulse was cutting a broad swath of destruction through the galaxy. Some planets escaped with just the total obliteration of all living things, no matter how primitive, but several planets suffered a much worse fate. Those with a molten core reacted to the pulse like an egg in a microwave. They boiled from the inside out and literally exploded.

The direction of the radiation pulse was in line with the plane of the solar system's planets and would hit Pluto first. Some of the other scientists who had been brought into the project expressed concern over the pulse's effect on the moon and other planetary bodies in the solar system. The Chulosians said the effect on the other planets and the sun would be negligible. But since only Hank knew of the Chulosians' remarkable abilities, these assurances did little to quell their fears.

"Excuse me, Doctor McDaniels. Please stand here," Crayto Shue-neenee thought-spoke.

McDaniels stepped to where the Chulosian directed him. The two groups formed into two circles: McDaniels, Devane, and Crayto in one group, with Hank, Leon, and Kamal Tarn in the other. The five remaining Chulosians split up between the groups. General Fisher and Libby stayed behind.

Proper clothing to withstand the cold was issued to everyone. The Chulosians declined, saying it was not required for them. They wore some type of covering that fitted them like a second skin.

The Chulosians became silent and then started the thought-merge humming sound they had made before. A clear bubble formed around each of the groups. It began to grow brighter and brighter until each sphere became a bright white opaque color. General Fisher and Libby backed away as the hum evoked a calm, peaceful feeling in them. Libby shivered as it made her tingle.

Suddenly the bubbles were gone and the light in the hangar returned to normal.

"Well, I guess they're on their way, Libby," the General said.

"They're already there," she replied, wondering how she knew that.

***

Once the Chulosians had left, everyone remaining breathed a sigh of relief. The President boarded Air Force One for the trip back to Washington along with the other politicians and the Joint Chiefs. General Reynolds stayed behind. He was driving back to China Lake. Two men waited for him in his staff car.

"Did you get the video tape?" the General asked.

"Yes, sir," one of the men answered.

He pulled a cassette tape from his coat pocket and showed it to the General.

"You understand your orders, gentlemen? I want this tape distributed to the media at exactly 4:30 p.m. I have a little surprise planned for our Chulosian visitors."

"Yes, sir, General. We have an appointment at the CNN studios in Los Angeles at 4:30. It will be the lead story on the five o'clock news."

"Thank you, gentlemen."

The General's pleasure was genuine as he contemplated the results of this leak.

30

A s Libby had told the General, Hank and his team arrived at the North pole site almost instantaneously. Leon was fascinated with the Chulosian sphere and tried to figure out how it worked. He thought it was amazing that the sphere could simply dissolve around them like an early morning fog on a summer day. He couldn't see any moving parts. In fact, he thought, it almost seemed to be alive. He would have to add this to the long list of questions he wanted to ask the Chulosians. The group proceeded to the site of the Pulsar Fence antennas.

It really was like a fence, Hank saw. Several structures about eight feet tall, each made up of antenna arrays circled a twenty-foot diameter satellite dish: it was a fence of specially designed plastic-coated metal rods. Leon thought it looked like a big round hair comb. At the edge of the site were the portable generating stations that supplied the unit with electrical power.

The site at the South Pole was identical except that the system there required two satellite dishes due to the trajectory of the radiation pulse. Because of the angle of the Earth, the pulse would hit the South Pole first as it traveled past the planet. The two sets of arrays would charge the particles in the atmosphere as the pulsar field oscillated back and forth at tremendous speed from pole to pole. The result of this game of atmospheric ping-pong would be an impenetrable force field of energy that would prevent any of the radiation from striking the Earth. It would literally bounce off.

Kamal Tarn and the other Chulosians were satisfied that their instructions for the construction of the fence had been followed to the letter. They thought-merged with Hank.

"It is well done, Hank Stanton. The fence your people have constructed here will work. When can we perform a test of the installation?" Kamal asked.

"As soon as we contact the other station at the South Pole. We must synchronize the test in order to start the reciprocal motion of microwaves from pole to pole. Once this is done, the field strength of the Pulsar Fence will be tested at various points around the planet. I will call my fellow scientists and tell them to begin," Hank said.

He picked up a special cellular phone and punched in the three digit code for McDaniels and his South Pole team.

"Hello, Brian, this is Hank Stanton. Are we ready to begin the test?"

"Yes, Hank. We're ready here," McDaniels replied.

"Okay. Begin the countdown on my mark. Ten, nine, eight, seven, six, five..."

Chulosians and humans on both teams waited in silent anticipation as Hank continued the countdown.

"...four, three, two, one. Energize."

At the South Pole, Brian McDaniels and Edward Devane sat at the controls in the mobile nuclear power unit. They engaged the power couplings and energized the system. They heard the low whine of the power turbines getting up to speed. As soon as the rpm gauge detected the system to be running at the correct revolutions, it would automatically engage the electronic distribution grid to power up the tower.

They paid close attention to the power distribution and the power output gauges. The two large satellite dishes were to send a blanket microwave band that would be received by the dish at the North Pole and returned to the South Pole.

Brian was the first to notice that something was wrong. The mobile power generating turbines were putting out more than enough power, but the broadcast beam was falling off.

"Brian, what's wrong?" Hank's voice came through on the cellular phone. "Your signal isn't reaching us. Check the tunable gain and see if you can boost the output. You may have to narrow the bandwidth."

"Hank, I don't understand this. We're at peak power right now, but the signal is being dissipated somehow. We're going to have to shut it down to try and find the failure. The Chulosians are all doing that mind-bonding thing. Maybe they can come up with the answer. I'll get back to you as soon as we have some news."

The Chulosians at the South Pole were thought-merging with their counterparts at the North Pole. Brian thought it was nothing short of supernatural that these creatures could actually speak to each other over such long distances. The mental conversation they engaged in was over in less than a minute. Crayto Shueneenee approached Brian and said, "We must inspect the power junction conduit. The failure is there."

"The power junction conduit?" Brian asked. "I hope the problem isn't there. It's the only one we have. In fact, it was fabricated specifically to carry a generated output of ten gigawatts. Let's go. We don't have any time to waste."

They stepped out of the heated mobile station and walked up the path to the antenna array. A small, stainless steel shed housed the power junction conduit designed to join the cables together that powered the two microwave dishes. Brian knew something was wrong the second he approached the power shed. He could feel the heat radiating from it even before he opened the door.

As Brian pulled the shed doors back on their hinges, thick black smoke billowed from the small electrical room, the acrid smell of burning insulation filling his nostrils. Brian waved his hand in the room to clear some of the smoke. The system had been powered down so it was safe to get a close look at what happened. Everyone crowded around the small room trying to see what damage had been done.

The power couplings at the four junctions had fused together from the tremendous power generated by the turbines. Brian couldn't believe his eyes as he gazed at the molten and fused cables. Defeated, he stood up and walked away from the building.

"Edward, it's hopeless. We got those couplings from JPL. They're the only ones in existence. It'll take days to fabricate new ones, and we have less than thirty-six hours. What are we going to do?" Brian asked his colleague, dropping to his knees in frustration and exhaustion.

The Chulosians examined the shed and thought-merged amongst themselves and with the others at the North Pole. If they had a solution, Brian thought, they'd better come up with it quickly. The world was running out of time.

***

At the other end of the Earth, Kamal Tarn approached Hank and told him it would be necessary for the team to go to the South Pole. They would attempt to rebuild the power unit there.

"Hank Stanton, we will create a Chulosian crystal fiber to act as a new conduit for the power machine. We can use the particles of your frozen ocean to fabricate it. Come. We must go to the others."

Kamal and the other Chulosians gathered into a circle and Hank joined them. He instructed Leon to stay behind and monitor the Pulsar Fence array. The Chulosian sphere formed around the small group and in an instant they arrived at the South Pole site. The sphere quickly dissolved and was gone. The group was greeted by McDaniels and they proceeded to inspect the melted couplings.

"Kamal, this place is nothing but ice and snow," Hank said, gesturing with his arms that there wasn't much of anything else in Antarctica.

Kamal Tarn didn't seem to be concerned. One of the Chulosians stepped away from the rest of the group and began to walk in a circle. Hank and the others watched as the hard snow under their feet began to melt. The other Chulosians formed a circle and began to walk in the opposite direction. The snow began to melt faster until they were all standing in a pool of water. Suddenly a sphere formed within the circle and began to grow cloudy inside as if it were filling up with milk.

When the sphere was completely full, it began to grow brighter as the Chulosians circled it and made the humming sound of communal thought-merging. As the bubble of milky water glowed with greater intensity, the humming sound became more and more melodic. Hank thought it sounded almost like the Chulosians were singing. Then it stopped and the sphere began to grow smaller and smaller until it was the size of a basketball. The other scientists were completely baffled at what the aliens might be doing. On the edge of the merge, Hank knew vaguely what they were doing but the details eluded him.

Kamal Tarn walked over and picked up the small globe and then dropped it on the icy ground. It shattered like a piece of glass but within it was some kind of coiled twine. Kamal picked it up and brought it to the scientists. He held it out for them to see. Brian said it looked like fishing line. Edward didn't dare hazard a guess.

Hank took it from Kamal and saw that it looked like strands of fiber optic cable. Hank was close in his assumption. Kamal explained it was the power-carrying fiber that they needed. It would allow unlimited energy to flow to the fence, but would not get hot or burn. Hank handed the coil of fibers to Brian who took them with a look of wonder on his face.

"What do you know? A glass-like fiber that won't get hot or burn and made from snow? I'd say it's nothing short of amazing," Brian said. "All I can say is it had better work or we'll all be getting pretty damned hot around here, and the rest of the world too."

Kamal thought-merged with Hank, "It would be better if we installed the strands ourselves."

Hank relayed this to Brian who handed the strands back to Kamal. The Chulosian group circled the power coupling shed and went to work.

***

General Fisher received the report of the power failure from the South Pole and prayed that the Chulosian solution would work. Time was fast running out. There were already reports of high radiation counts at the higher elevations in the Southern Hemisphere.

Libby and Hank were able to speak privately on the satlink for only a minute. He told her he loved her and promised to return to Vandenberg tomorrow—if there *is* a tomorrow.

Libby reflected on the irony: The future of the entire world was in the hands of a group of aliens that only a handful of people even knew existed. Libby thought of the billions of people on the planet blissfully unaware of the catastrophe just hours away. They were all busy making love, making war, having babies, or murdering each other—all the things that seem so important and yet are so trivial when the entire human race is facing total annihilation.

It seemed so unfair. She and Hank had both had unhappy marriages because they'd both been married to their work. They'd finally found each other and fallen in love. And now this.

Kamal and the other Chulosians spent almost three hours replacing the burned out cables with the new glass fibers. When it was completed, Hank and the others looked at what the Chulosians had done. They were in awe at the technological masterpiece. The aliens had connected each fiber to the network of circuits that powered the Pulsar Fence array.

They were ready to test the system again. This time Hank knew it would work. Hank placed all of his hope in the science of the Chulosians and the power of the GEE.

Kamal Tarn and the other aliens crowded around the mobile power trailer and watched as Brian McDaniels prepared to energize the fence again. Hank contacted Leon Beardsley and informed him to fire up the North Pole array on his countdown.

Monitoring stations around the world were watching to see if the fence would work, waiting and wondering. Would the force field of energized particles in the upper atmosphere repel the approaching radiation storm?

Brian began the countdown again. Hank had his fingers crossed in the pockets of his parka.

"...three, two, one. Here goes."

Brian punched the buttons to start up the Pulsar Fence. The turbines whined up to a scream as they generated the gigawatts of power required to energize the pulsar array. The scientists checked the gauges as the antenna dishes broadcast a wide energy beam of microwaves that encircled the Earth and were amplified at the North Pole. The radio began picking up the transmissions of the monitoring stations calling in. Leon came on the radio and told them what they had all been waiting to hear: The shield was on-line.

A loud cheer rose up from the human scientists, and Hank noticed the Chulosians standing in a semi-circle with their mouths wide open. He was the first to stroke the tongues of the Chulosian delegation as the others followed suit. All they could do now was wait. The radiation pulse would strike in less than twenty-four hours and that would be the ultimate test.

$$***$$

Two men entered the office of CNN news director, Franklin Evans, and gave him a tape.

They sat there in silence as Evans watched the video monitor, his eyes as big as saucers. "Is this some kind of a hoax?"

"I can assure you, Mister Evans, that this comes straight from the General himself. He said you could be trusted to get this on the air."

"Well, you just tell the General that I owe him one for this. My God! How long did the President think he could keep a story like this from the American people? From the world?" He leaned over to the VCR and rewound the tape. He then jumped behind his desk and punched the intercom. "Jeffrey! Get your butt in here. NOW!" he yelled.

Seconds later a young man knocked on the door.

"Jeffrey. Get in here!"

Evans walked over to the VCR and took the video tape out of the unit and handed it to Jeffrey. "Take this up to the control room and tell Sam to get it cued. Then tell everyone I want a meeting on the studio floor in three minutes. Now GO!" he yelled.

"Mister Evans, we'll be going now. Thank you for your time." The two men rose to leave.

"You're thanking me? It's me who should be thanking you. This is the greatest story since Moses parted the Red Sea. Thank you, gentlemen. Thank you and General Reynolds."

31

News of the Chulosian visit to Earth hit the air waves at exactly 5:00. p.m. Pacific time. It was picked up by every station in the country and within an hour of the broadcast it was all over the world. Footage of the Chulosians standing with the President of the United States in an airplane hangar at Vandenberg Air Force Base was seen around the planet. Questions were asked in Congress and the President was besieged with requests to go on national television to make a statement.

The President called his closest advisors to the Oval Office for a meeting. He vowed that heads would roll for the premature release of the video, but they all knew it was too late to back out. What the President needed now was damage control. The news had told the world that a blast of radiation was going to strike the Earth in less than twenty-four hours. The President had hoped to stall for time, but that luxury was now gone. His advisors chattered like a bunch of old hens while the President prayed that the Pulsar Fence would work.

***

Hank Stanton and Kamal Tarn were relieved that everything was working. They had confidence that the Pulsar Fence would withstand the approaching radiation. They decided that the group would split up into three teams, one at each of the poles and a third back at Vandenberg to provide comlinks with other monitoring stations around the world. Hank and Kamal returned to California while Crayto and two other Chulosians returned to the North Pole to assist Leon. McDaniels and Devane along with the other Chulosians remained at the South Pole.

Hank and the others arrived at Vandenberg and the General and Libby were there to greet them. Hank emerged from the Chulosian travel sphere and instantly Libby had her arms around his neck. Kamal stood, mouth wide open, nodding his head in a display of Chulosian approval.

General Fisher broke the news to them about the broadcast, suggesting that they all go to the base's underground command center to discuss what should be done. They left the hangar and drove to the Operations Room. It was very similar to the Ops Room at the Cape except that it was almost five hundred feet underground.

General Fisher had his people set up a special area as living quarters for the Chulosians. The base personnel had all been ordered to remain silent about the unusual visitors. Their presence on Earth was supposed to be classified but now that everyone on the planet knew about them, the General was even more concerned for their safety. He had them segregated from the rest of the military personnel in a secured section of the underground command post, with six MPs assigned to provide around-the-clock protection.

One of the officers in the detail, a lieutenant named Bill Harsted, seemed more than a little uncomfortable protecting the visitors from Chulos. A shape-changing Eltorum, he had been on this planet for only a short time to observe the Chulosians and report back to General Reynolds. He knew by reputation that they were dangerous to the Eltorum, but had never actually seen a Chulosian before. He was unaware that they could probe the minds of others.

The Chulosians immediately recognized the Eltorum. They looked into his mind and knew the entire plan of their arch-enemy. They also saw the image of General Arthur Reynolds in his thoughts. As they probed the Eltorum's mind, his ability to maintain human appearance waned and he slowly changed back into reptilian form. Lieutenant Harsted was shocked when he realized what the Chulosians were doing to him, and before he lost his shape-shifting powers completely, he deserted his post.

The Chulosians continued to thought-merge throughout the day. Hank thought it best to leave them alone and went off to spend some time with Libby. Later, he and Libby had dinner with General Fisher to discuss what they thought might happen after the radiation pulse passed by the planet.

"Hank, the President is going to hold a news conference in an hour. The decision now rests with him," the General said.

"The world will have to be told the truth about the Chulosians, General. These beings have a great deal to share with us. Our science alone could be advanced a thousand years by some of the things I've seen."

The discussion centered around how they could introduce the Chulosians to the rest of the world without creating an uproar. It was a perplexing question. General Fisher hoped the President could handle it.

"I know that your argument is a good one, Doctor Stanton, but we must consider the rest of society as well," the General said. "Now that the world knows of their existence, what affect will the announcement about the Chulosians have on the religious leaders of the world and the millions of people who believe in what they say? Will it shatter their belief in God or strengthen it? What about the world's economy? Will it be completely disrupted by the possibility of fantastic new discoveries? Already the news of the Chulosians has created mass hysteria and chaos. We must carefully consider these questions and choose our path wisely in the days ahead. But first we have to survive tomorrow."

The President's news conference was about what Hank expected. He acknowledged the existence of the Chulosians and implored everyone to stay calm. He played down the radiation pulse and the aliens. He said they were our friends. What else could he do.

They finished their dinner and the General excused himself for the evening. Quarters had been prepared for Hank and Libby, but neither of them felt like retiring for the day. Hand in hand, they walked through the underground expanse of the air base, talking about their future and what it held for each of them. Hank stopped in a small deserted alcove and pulled Libby to him.

"You know, Libby, these past few months have been wildly strange and hectic. Through it all, I've felt that you were always there waiting for me. I like that feeling and would like it to go on forever. When all this is over, will you marry me?" He blushed and shuffled his feet like a high school kid asking a girl to dance at the prom.

Libby looked Hank in the face, took both his hands and gave him a big kiss. "Yes. I would love to be Mrs. Hank Stanton." She pulled him closer and kissed him again.

They spent the night making love and planning a future neither of them was sure of. They awoke the next morning entwined in each other's arms and made love again. They held on to each other in silence, knowing that in less than four hours the radiation pulse would strike Earth.

The storm surge from the radiation pulse could begin at any moment. Everyone involved with the Pulsar Fence was cautiously optimistic that it would hold. The orbiting satellite weather detection systems were their first line of defense. The satellites would detect the approaching radiation storm, but being outside the protection of the fence, they would either be knocked out or explode into tiny fragments of space debris.

Around the world, entire populations had been told to stay indoors. Since the announcement had been made about the Chulosians and the radiation storm approaching Earth, people had had little time to react or prepare. The effect on the Earth's population had been downplayed by governments and the media in order to avoid mass panic. It didn't work. Fringe religious groups held all-night vigils. Other groups held all-night orgies. And, of course, looting and burning raged out of control all across the planet.

***

When the radiation pulse hit the Earth's atmosphere full force, the sky lit up all over the planet like a fireworks display. The shock wave of the blast caused a disturbance in the gravitational pull between the Earth and the Moon. Hundred-foot waves raced to the Pacific Rim coasts as an undersea earthquake shifted the ocean floor. A volcano erupted in Japan and the desert floor of California was rocked by a 7.2 temblor that devastated Bakersfield. Oddly the San Andreas fault held, sparing Los Angeles and San Francisco.

The underground command center at Vandenberg suffered only minor damage from the California quake, but everyone was shaken.

Hank tried to reach Leon at the North Pole but all communications were knocked out. The Chulosians, however, were silently thought-merging with the rest of their group and were well aware of what was taking place around the world.

The Pulsar Fence had worked. Around the planet, the devastation was relatively minor; fatalities came in at less than one million world-wide. The outer atmospheric radiation level was returning to normal levels and the radiation pulse had passed the planet as it coursed through the solar system. A loud cheer went up throughout the command center as the General and Hank went to the Chulosian quarters to congratulate them and thank them for their help. There, they met Doctor McDaniels, Professor Devane, and Leon emerging with the delegation from Chulos.

Kamal Tarn and the other Chulosians circled the group of humans, open-mouthed and nodding their heads. Hank and the others stroked their tongues and Libby even gave Kamal a very human kiss on the side of his head which pleasantly surprised the Chulosian. His skin displayed a kaleidoscope of colors in pleasure.

But for Hank, the ceremony was marred by a serious concern. The threat of global destruction had passed, but the question of what to tell the world about the Chulosians still nagged at him. He saw that it was also on the General's mind when one of the General's aides approached and handed him a message. He read it quickly and then called for silence in the room.

"Everyone, please, may I have your attention? I have just received a report that the radiation pulse has apparently either knocked out or destroyed every man-made satellite in orbit. This news has been confirmed by independent observatories around the world. Other than land lines, all communication links are down."

Only Hank and Leon knew what this catastrophe meant. If the Hubble was out of action, the Chulosians were stranded on Earth.

Hank thought-merged with the Chulosians but before he could ask them if they realized what this meant, the thoughts of Kamal penetrated his mind.

"Hank Stanton, this news is not troubling to my people. We have a way to return to our home world. We will construct a Corbal Ring here in this place. With it we will be able to return to Chulos. You know the power of the Corbal Ring, Hank. You have seen it on our world so it cannot be left behind for the Eltorum Shayloree that reside on Earth. They will use its power to bring destruction to your people and eventually others. It must not be allowed to happen."

"The Eltorum?" Hank asked. "Kamal, who are the Eltorum?"

Kamal thought-merged with him. "They have been on your world for many years. It is not their purpose to bring knowledge to your world. It is only for the enslavement of Earth people. The Eltorum are a dying race and they must mix their genetics with those of your people in order to remain alive. They have been absorbing people on your planet for many years. They are an enemy to Chulos and to all the worlds that are members of the Circle of Planets, as Earth must now become."

Hank was surprised to hear Kamal speak of an alien race already on Earth. It sounded like a sinister invasion. Everyone in NASA was aware of the countless reports of sightings and the rampant alien abduction rumors. Hank now wondered if perhaps it might all be true.

"How can I recognize the Eltorum?" Hank asked.

"Hank Stanton, you have the power of the GEE. You will see through their false identities and you will be the one to lead your people and cast them from your planet. They know that we are here. Soon they will learn that you have the power of thought-merging. As soon as Earth has joined in the Circle of Planets they will leave. They will not be able to survive thought-merging.

They are like chameleons and can change their shape into the appearance of anything they touch. Many of your world's inhabitants have been taken by them. They are the grey ones and the reptilians. They have taken many shapes, each from a different world they have enslaved. They are the ones that many from your world have been speaking of. They falsely appear as friends, as the holders of the light of truth. But the Eltorum are darkness. We have battled them before, Hank Stanton, here on this planet."

Hank was perplexed. He needed to know more about this alien race who had been secretly coexisting on Earth undetected. Kamal placed a thought image in Hank's mind and he understood. The

Chulosians and their ancestors were the light beings of our past. Our mythology, scriptures, and all the stories that had been passed down through the ages had been perverted. The Chulosians were the promise of the future. It was they who told our ancestors about the time of the awakening and now the time had finally come.

"Hank, it is time for us to return to Chulos. After we depart, you must place this globe inside the ring," Kamal said, handing him a small crystal.

Hank realized the depth of responsibility that Kamal entrusted to him. He never felt so honored yet so humble in his life. Hank agreed and promised to see that the Corbal Ring was destroyed as soon as they were gone.

Kamal sensed the feeling of loss within Hank. He told Hank that the Chulosians would not be gone for long. They would be able to communicate with Earth in a way that didn't require the Hubble as the conduit. Although Hank understood what Kamal said, he wondered how long it would be before they would meet again. The Chulosians completed the Corbal Ring in the center of the hangar.

As the Chulosians worked, Hank took the General on one side. "General, the Corbal Ring is technology centuries beyond ours, and the Chulosians feel that leaving it here would interfere with the balance on our planet."

The General disagreed. "But we can't let them take it. How are we going to communicate with them? It's the doorway to Chulos and we must keep it open."

"General," Hank replied, "the Chulosians aren't the only extraterrestrials currently on this planet. A group called the Eltorum, or Greys, is also here. And the Chulosians are adamant that the Ring must not fall into their hands."

Having been privy to some of the speculation about ETs already, General Fisher understood and, after more persuasion by Hank, reluctantly agreed.

The Chulosians stood in a circle and faced outward toward everyone. Kamal stood before Hank and opened his mouth. Hank walked up to him and stroked his tongue. They thought-merged as Kamal spoke in mind pictures to Hank. He told Hank that the power of the GEE would direct his actions from now on.

"We will be together again soon, Hank Stanton, on Chulos. I have given you a great gift that you will learn to use for the benefit of all Earth's people. *Chetar MarfynGee Golesco.* You stand within the Circle of Light and the Circle of Light will surround you forever."

Kamal and the others turned to face inward. The Corbal Ring began to hum as the Cotera Tunnel vortex appeared. The Chulosians began thought-merging as the vortex grew larger and larger until it finally engulfed them in the Globe of Oreth. In a flash of light they were gone.

Hank stepped into the Corbal Ring and placed the small crystal Kamal had given him in the center. Everyone in the room stepped back as the ring began shaking and emitting a strange noise. They watched in amazement as the Corbal Ring became transparent and then just disappeared in front of them. The Chulosians had pulled it through with them.

As they stood there, Hank felt an image come into his mind, a thought picture from Kamal Tarn: "Trusted Friend." He'd just been tested and passed. The thought caused him to smile.

Libby came up to him and put her arm around his waist. "What is it, Hank?" she asked.

"Oh, I was just thinking of Kamal Tarn and the other Chulosians, wondering if we'll ever see them again," Hank said, smiling.

They walked hand-in-hand out of the hangar and into the daylight. Hank sent a thought picture to Kamal Tarn on the planet Chulos. In an instant just one word traveled 27 light years across the galaxy.

"Brothers."

***

The confetti and rice flew as Hank and Libby ran toward the limo, bound in their love for each other, and now celebrities around the world. Everyone cheered as they ducked into the long white car. As soon as the door was closed, Hank and Libby were locked in a deep embrace in the back seat. Within a minute, they were naked and making love. They had found that the GEE amplified every aspect of human experience and sex was no exception. In fact, the GEE took their love-making to levels that few people could even imagine.

For both of them it was a dream come true: the Prince and the Princess riding off to live happily ever after.

***

General Fisher took everyone by surprise with an unprecedented move. He revealed everything about the Chulosians to the world press. It didn't take long for world religious leaders to come barking for proof and the "truth." With their followers demanding honesty and clarity, their positions as leaders of the faithful throughout the world were in jeopardy. Both leaders and followers wanted the truth and they wanted it immediately; their limited view of reality had been smashed wide open and the very fabric of their lives was in shreds. For millions of others, however, the joy of knowing that extraterrestrial life and friendship existed beyond Earth inspired them. But many of these people began to worship the Chulosians as gods, and even the ET supporters splintered off into warring factions.

Many people were angered to know that their government and religious leaders had tried to suppress the knowledge of the Chulosians. General Reynolds found himself on the wrong side, and his entire operation at the China Lake Mine was in jeopardy. His only salvation would be to convince the President that the Chulosians were not the friendly and benevolent beings they claimed to be, but were actually the enemy of the whole human race. They had misrepresented themselves as gods, he claimed, and their appearance on Earth was mistakenly being seen by many as the "Second Coming."

The General's timing was perfect. Global chaos was increasing exponentially. The President was besieged by other world leaders to take the lead and restore order to the civilized world. The President and his advisors debated long into the night. Should they welcome the aliens as saviors and open their arms to them, or condemn them as a global threat and close the door on them?

With the presidential election looming, it all boiled down to votes. His advisors persuaded the President that more votes would be won if the United States circled its wagons against the Chulosians. Then the country would rally behind the President and sweep him back into office. Therefore, he spoke out against the Chulosians. The world was told a lie. The Chulosians were branded as an enemy of the human race, and apart from a brief statement, all reference to them was quashed by the mass media. The independent press, however, had a field day with the reversal. No one knew what was truth or lies.

People who were initially elated at the news of the friendly extra-terrestrials were now offended to hear government and religious leaders coming out in force against them. Protests and counter-protests erupted everywhere. Religious leaders demanded that action be taken against the supporters of the ungodly extraterrestrials. In many cities, the National Guard was called in to maintain law and order. Hotbeds of radical activity, such as Berkeley, suffered major damage, with entire city blocks burned to the ground. Buses and trains were fire-bombed and thousands of innocent citizens were killed or injured.

The radiation storm that nearly destroyed life on the planet was soon forgotten as old political rivalries and religious bigotry surfaced stronger than ever. The religions of the world had become unstable as their stranglehold on superstitions and outmoded beliefs of the people they controlled fell apart. How could they compete with the existence of these devils from another world?

The climate of division disrupted everything. Around the world, stock markets crashed and left the economy in shambles. The world's military leaders found that they too were being drawn into the chaos. The division between those for and against the Chulosians reached a fever pitch. In just a few weeks, the world systems fell apart.

General Reynolds and the Eltorum leader, Sataran, couldn't have planned a world situation any better. Soon the planet would be in such a state of confusion that it would be easy for a relatively small military contingent to step in and take control of the planet. Slavery of the entire human race was just a short step away.

Craig Williams, now working with General Reynolds at The Mine, figured he could play a pivotal role in the General's quest for world domination. The Eltorum had promised the General he would rule the planet once it was under their control. Craig was reinstated as the mission director at NASA, and in the ensuing chaos, General Reynolds had all charges against him dropped.

General Reynolds spoke out on national television. He lied and said that the Chulosians had abandoned the human race. They were gone and would never return. He knew that if he and the Eltorum could mobilize quickly, planet Earth would be theirs before anyone realized what had happened.

There was only one problem and it had to be dealt with once and for all.

***

Hank and Libby were at home in Maryland when Leon called. Libby answered the phone. "Libby, quick, turn on the television," he said.

"What is it, Leon?"

"It's Craig Williams. He's back at the Center. He's holding a news conference right now."

"Okay, Leon. Hold on."

Libby grabbed the remote from the bedside table and switched on the TV. The news conference was on every channel. She turned up the volume.

"Hank, come here quickly!" she yelled.

Hank, in the kitchen making coffee, ran into the bedroom, alarmed at Libby's tone. "What's the matter, Libby?"

"Hank. It's that bastard Craig Williams. He's holding a news conference at Goddard. He's talking about you."

Hank took the remote and turned up the volume.

"... and Doctor Hank Stanton is responsible for all this. He has denied the existence of God in favor of these aliens. He has turned his back on our country and the world. He should not be allowed to live among decent, God-fearing people."

"What the hell is this shit? That asshole can't get away with this! The bastard's lying. Libby, what the hell can we do about this?"

"Libby! Libby! You still there?" Leon yelled into the phone.

"Oh, geez. I forgot about Leon," she said, handing the phone to Hank.

"Hi, Leon. Did you catch that bullshit on the tube?"

"Doc, Doc, listen. Didn't Kamal Tarn tell you about the grey guys? What did he call 'em? Eltor something?"

"Leon, you're absolutely right!" A whole scenario to deal with this situation suddenly formed in Hank's mind, complete in all the details. Thank heavens for the GEE, Hank thought.

Hank grabbed Libby around the waist and gave her a big hug. Their eyes met and Libby felt the heat surge up in every cell, this time infused with intense sexual energy. Hank felt it, too and they kissed passionately as they ripped each other's clothes off for the third time that day.

"Hey! Will you guys cool off for one minute, please," Leon yelled into the phone again. This time Libby picked up the receiver.

"Sorry, Leon. It's the GEE. Sometimes it gets pretty intense."

"The GEE? Yeah, right, the GEE. Would someone please tell me what the GEE is?"

Libby and Hank thought-merged and on the other end of the phone line, Leon saw Hank's and Libby's combined thought pictures in his mind. The entire answer was there.

Hank took the receiver from Libby and spoke to Leon. "The Eltorum will soon be powerless, Leon. They can't assimilate the GEE. Soon everyone on earth who has welcomed the Chulosians in their hearts and minds will be untouchable and invincible. The Eltorum will be powerless and will have to leave the planet."

"That sounds great, Doc, but what about Craig Williams? In case you didn't hear, he just about branded you the AntiChrist. You won't be able to show your face in public."

"I won't have to, Leon."

Libby looked at him and smiled. "Should I pack a bag?" she asked.

"Doc, I don't understand. What do you mean, 'You won't have to'?" Leon asked.

"Leon, by tonight, Libby and I will be on Chulos. You better come over right away. Libby and I have a gift we'd like to give you."

***

Hank and Libby arrived on Chulos as guests of Kamal Tarn and the Council of Circles. For both of them it was a second honeymoon. They spent their time exploring the planet and learning the ways of the GEE. The Chulosians welcomed them wherever they traveled throughout the planet. They learned all about the Chulosian people and how they cherished and protected the lesser planets throughout the universe. The power of the GEE was all encompassing. The power of the light was everywhere. Libby felt as though she were in heaven.

***

On Earth, Leon was busy. He used the gift wisely, seeking out those who had heard the tone of the awakening. It began slowly. One initiated ten. Ten initiated a hundred. They in turn initiated a thousand.

Soon the hearts and minds of millions of people were open to the GEE. That which the chaos had lain waste was rebuilt, but on a totally different foundation: loving cooperation with the GEE. The Eltorum interfered where they could, but it was a losing battle. Because they couldn't understand why someone would do anything to help another, they didn't know how to prevent it and watched helplessly as communities came together based on love and cooperation.

***

Hank saw everything that was happening on Earth. The Corbal Ring was a window on the universe. He saw the Eltorum and those who followed them. He thought-merged with Kamal and asked him how long it would be before the GEE made the Eltorum leave the planet.

"It is up to you, Hank. You will return to Earth and be the one to lead your people against them. The GEE has made you strong. The Earth has been chosen as the battleground for the final conflict between the darkness of the Eltorum and the light of the GEE. Soon your planet will be rid of them. And everyone that embraces the GEE will be free of limitation, able to travel the universe as we do, *forever.*"

GLOSSARY

Chulos: The fourth planet orbiting the star Vega. Distance from Earth, 27 light years. Home world of the Chulosians. Oxygen-enriched liquid (water) atmosphere. The entire civilization of Chulos lives in the sea. No land mass on the planet.

Chulosians: Inhabitants of the planet Chulos, dolphin-like, amphibious humanoid beings. An advanced race and culture, they can exist in an air-breathing atmosphere for extended periods. The Chulosians are a race of explorers who search the galaxy for other life-forms. They are many years ahead of Earth in science and technology. The Chulosians use bio-mechanics—living organisms—instead of mechanical devices. They speak by thought-merging and can travel great distances in outer space in a short period of time by harnessing interstellar gravity waves. They can also project thoughts and images through space and time by use of the Corbal Ring of Infinity.

Corbal Ring of Infinity: A bio-mechanical device that enhances the thought-merging process of the Chulosians. It can assemble a thought as a holographic image and project it anywhere in the known universe immediately. The Chulosians use the Corbal Ring as a means of examining new worlds before attempting to explore them physically. With the Globe of Oreth as an environmental chamber, the Chulosians can enter the Corbal Ring and project themselves anywhere in the known universe.

Circle of Comastyr: The family house of Kamal Tarn. All of the families of Chulos belong to circles called Chotor that are all members of the primary circle that governs Chulos. There are 28 circles on Chulos. Every Chulosian is a member of one of the circles.

Chotor: Each circle of Chulos is comprised of member families. Each individual family is called a Chotor. Kamal Tarn is the head of his Chotor, in the Circle of Comastyr.

Cotera Tunnel: The vortex of light and travel within the Corbal Ring of Infinity that allows thought and material travel throughout the universe.

Circle of the Gee, The Council of Circles: The governing circle of the planet Chulos that directs the thought-merging and activities of its inhabitants on a planet-wide scale. Directs all outer world exploration and the welcoming of new worlds into the great circle of friendship. Each house, or Chotor, is represented on the Council. The Circle of the Gee which is comprised of the same members, is responsible for the direction of the energy force that flows through every Chulosian. The Circle of the Gee is not a religion as Earth people might characterize it, but a natural, spiritual force the Chulosians have been able to harness for the benefit of themselves and others.

The GEE: The name the Chulosians have given to the invisible force of energy that allows them to thought-merge, travel among the planets and harness the living energy of their planet and others.

Circle of Barsin-Gee: A prominent circle on Chulos. They are the caretakers of Chulos.

Crikodynke: A Chulosian Pulsar Fence. A force field array that is used to replenish the ozone layer in a planet's outer atmosphere. It can repel the radiation bursts of dying stars that travel throughout the galaxy.

Cremboseedee: Close friend, confidant and assistant.

Crayto Shooneenee: Close friend of Kamal Tarn. Scientist and member of the Circle of Comastyr.

Craytoll Kooblund: A window into other worlds. Used by the Chulosians as a non-invasive tool which allows study of other civilizations in order to determine if they are benign or hostile. Used with the Corbal Ring of Infinity.

The Craytoll Segment: A distant corner of the Dralorum Galaxy composed of many Outer Rock Worlds being studied by the Chulosians. The planets Melkos–3 and Eltorum are located in this area of space.

Circle of Dilothan: Outer Rock World explorers of Chulos. One of the oldest Chotors on Chulos.

Crikodynee of Karmosh: A thought test used by the Chulosians to probe the inner self in order to identify a person's true feelings.

Alpore-Tem: The home city of the Circle of Comastyr.

Bosenjoe Marluca: Member of the Council of Circles and the Circle of the Gee. Speaker for the Chotor of Cloresnee.

Eltor: A rock world in the Dralorum Galaxy, and home of a species known as the Eltorium Shaybree.

Eltorum Shayloree: Advanced rock worlders who are like humanoid chameleons. They can disguise their appearance for short periods of time. Those of Earth's people who have seen them in their true state call them 'Greys.' They have been influencing events on Earth for years. They are a dying race and are the enemies of the Chulosians and the GEE. They have been absorbing Earth's people by merging their biology and creating hybrids. They cannot withstand the thought power of the GEE. It is the only force that can expose them.

"Chetar MarfynGee Golesco": An ancient Chulosian saying that means "You stand within the Circle of Light, and the Circle of Light will surround you forever."

BarseldwynGee: Podor or speaker for the Council of Circles.

Podor: The primary speaker of each Chotor on Chulos.

Clonar: A star in the Craytoll Segment of the galaxy that has gone supernova.

Gee-Corem: Home city of the Circle of the Gee and Council of Circles.

Keltor Cremboseedee: Head of the Circle of Dilothan and member of the Council of Circles at Gee-Corem.

Chulosian Time Partor: A segment of time set aside for the 'awakening' of founding worlds. It is the time allotted by the Chulosians for a world to come to an understanding of the GEE.

Habadasor Elnee: A tool used by the Chulosians to infuse the physical power of the GEE into an alien and allow them to survive the liquid atmosphere of Chulos.

Lector of Ramoth: A symbolic title given to Outer Rock Worlders who have been brought into the Circle of the GEE and given a place on the Council of Circles. Its actual translation means 'First Brother of Chulos and Speaker of New Worlds.'

Lector: A representative from each circle and a speaker on the Council of Circles.

Taymal Kamashee: Life partner of Kamal Tarn. She is an explorer and botanist from the Circle of HofellowdwynGee.

Circle of HofellowdwynGee: The circle of a family of botanical explorers of Chulos. They discovered the plant worlds of the Malorum galaxy.

Malorum Galaxy: A group of 63 known worlds that trade with the planet Chulos and have abundant edible vegetation of all kinds.

The "Haven" Worlds: These are planets throughout the explored universe that have embraced the knowledge and power of the GEE.

Globe of Oreth: A bio-mechanical, living crystal used by the Chulosians to travel anywhere in the explored universe. It is also called The Sphere of Motion. It can contain the liquid atmosphere of Chulos.

Melkos–3: A rock world inhabited by barbaric, lizard-like aliens. Several Chulosian explorers perished on an expedition to Melkos–3. Travel there is forbidden.

Kamal Tarn: First member and Lector of the Circle of Comastyr. A scientist and explorer.

Relon & Relon Cretor: The time it takes the planet Chulos to orbit the star Vega. About three and half Earth years. A Relon Cretor is a specific time period established by the Chulosians. Because of Chulos's broad eliptical orbit, the Chulosians concept of time is much different from that of Earth.

Karsal Cremboseedee: First Lector of the Circle of the Gee. He holds the highest and most respected position on the Council of Circles.

Profor: The term used by Chulosians whenever they speak out loud. Amongst themselves, Chulosians usually thought-merge using mind pictures or images instead of words.

Traylocore: A translation device designed by the scientists of Chulos to assist themselves and others to speak and be understood.

Shoone: A Chulosian term for planets with benign intelligent lifeforms.

Pelnor: A planet of exile.

Shooneenee MarfaldwynGee: A member of the Chotor BorolenGee. They are the traders of Chulos. A prominent Lector on the Council of Circles.

Shoone Peltoran–3: The Chulosian words for planet Earth.

Sataran: Quadrant leader of the forces of the Eltorum Shayloree.

Vega: The blue/white star that gives life to Chulos. It is 27 light years from Earth.

Future Books from the Same Author...

ROCKWORLD: THE APOCALYPSE OF LIGHT

Earth is in an uproar of religious chaos and hypocrisy that rivals the Middle Ages. The population is divided into two camps: supporters of the Eltorum, an ancient species of invaders with a secret agenda—plunder of Earth's natural resources and enslavement of its human population—versus followers of the GEE, that mysterious lifeforce energy introduced to Earth by the Chulosians.

But will the people of Earth embrace the truth and accept the Chulosians, or will they deny the power of the GEE and witness for themselves the beginning of the end of the human race? In this *Second Book of The Chulosian Chronicles*, Hank leads a great battle and carves out a new destiny for himself and the entire human race.

CHULOS: THE ASCENSION

In this *Third Book of The Chulosian Chronicles*, humanity must now choose between joining the Circle of Planets or going it alone.

On Chulos, Libby's daughter Kaylota, shares her father's destiny. But is her awesome power enough to overcome the secret army pledged to seize control of planet Earth as the rest of the galaxy looks on.

SUBSCRIBE TO *THE GALACTIC OBSERVER*

The Galactic Observer, edited by author Lee Shargel, is full of information, news, and quotes that cannot be obtained from any other source. If you, or anyone you know, would like to subscribe to this cutting edge newsletter, send a check, and your name and address to: The Galactic Observer, PO Box 26893, Tamarac, FL 33320.

You can be ahead of the pack for only $12.00 a year, including mailing (Continental US only–overseas subscriptions: $24.00/year.) Still not sure? Check out back issues on the Internet at: *www.users1.ee.net/pmason* and choose *The Galactic Observer* link.

Got a UFO encounter story? E-mail Lee at lshargel1@aol.com.

OTHER BOOKS BY OUGHTEN HOUSE...

The Extraterrestrial Vision by Gina Lake tells us what we need to know about our extraterrestrial heritage. Through telepathic contact with the author, Theodore, a nonphysical entity, prepares us for direct contact with the various groups of ETs currently orbiting our planet. He details their various agendas, why they are here, what they expect of us, and what we can expect of them. — *ISBN 1-880666-19-7, $13.95*

ET Contact: The Next Step Revealed, by Gina Lake. Through telepathic contact with the author, the Confederation of Planets details the adjustments mankind must make, now and in the near future, to prepare for mass contact with ETs. The briefing covers such aspects of life after the landings as world government, redistribution of wealth and resources, embracing new technology, and changes in our welfare and education systems. *ET Contact* also reveals the changes that each of us must make as an individual in order to cohabit with our new neighbors. Get a head start on the necessary changes now with this indispensable guidebook on co-existing with ETs direct from the Confederation leadership. — *ISBN -880666-62-6, $12.95*

Eagles Wings is a bi-monthly magazine packed with the latest UFO, ET, and ascension information, and features material received telepathically from The Ashtar Command, Intergalactic Council, and many others involved in Earth's transformation. US subscription is only $27 per year (Canada and Mexico: $37).

FREE CATALOG

To order these and other fine titles direct from **Oughten House**, request a complete catalog, or be put on our mailing list, contact us:
- By phone at (888) ORDER IT (toll free) or (510) 447-2332
- By fax at (510) 447-2376
- By e-mail at oughtenhouse@rest.com
- Or in writing to: Oughten House Publications, PO Box 2008, Livermore, CA 94551, USA.